Narcissistic Personality Disorder

A Self-Help Recovery Emotional Guide to Understand the Causes of Narcissism and How to Survive Narcissistic Abuse in Any Kind of Relationship

By: Alison Care

ISBN: 9781073541102

Table of Contents

Introduction

Have you ever had a relationship with a narcissist? A parent, sibling, friend, or significant other? Can you recognize the signs of a narcissist? Some people pick up on them relatively quickly but some don't recognize the warning signs and that can end up being unfortunate for them.

In this book, Narcissistic Personality Disorder: A Self Help Recovery Emotional Guide to Understand the Causes of Narcissism and How to Survive Narcissistic Abuse in Any Kind of Relationship, you will learn just what a narcissistic personality order (NPD) is, what the specific signs of a person with NPD, how this personality disorder can be callous and destructive and how a person can become abused and traumatized by a person with this personality disorder.

Narcissists are initially very charming, clever, and even fun to be with. However, underneath this pleasant façade is someone who lacks empathy, feels they are "entitled" to be treated differently, feel that most people are not their equals, and believe they are superior.

The chapters that follow will give you an overview of the narcissistic
personality condition, as well as its causes, the signs and symptoms, the different types of NPD, and how to deal with a person who has a narcissistic personality.

This book is written to help people identify a person with NPD or if you are already in a relationship, to benefit from the resources provided to help you in dealing with a person who may be psychologically harmful to you and help you in dealing with them.

How to Get the Most Out of this Book

This book is written to work in a number of ways:

Read this book in its entirety to ensure that you fully understand the narcissistic personality disorder, what causes this type of disorder, the signs and symptoms, victims of narcissistic abuse, and how to deal with a person with NPD, or;

Use the book as a guide to help you review and reread portions of the book that you may feel pertains to you or someone you know.

This book will help you understand the effects that the narcissistic personality disorder has on a person when they have to deal with this disorder in their family life, friends, co-worker, a boss, or romantic relationship.

This book is written to be informative and instructional. Some of the information may be, for some, unbelievable and may wonder how someone can become involved with a person with NPD who can be so cruel and devalue a person of their own thoughts and their spirit.

However, once you read about what this disorder is about and how a person can be attracted and get involved with a person with NPD, it will become more understandable.

This book has been written in hopes that you learn about people who have a narcissistic personality disorder and how one can have a better understanding of the disorder.

Chapter 1: The Narcissistic Personality Disorder

Have you ever had a family member, spouse, friend, or business associate act as if the world revolves around them? Do you walk on eggshells when you are speaking with them because you need to cough every word, every phrase so as to not upset or anger them? Are you constantly expected to heap praise and point out all the supposed wonderful things they've done when in fact they haven't contributed as much as they think they have and when they do, the little that they think is so great and they expect to be thanked and congratulated for it again and again?

Is their mantra "It's all about me?" If all of this is familiar to you and you can immediately think of someone in your life that fits the bill, then you're dealing with a person with a narcissistic personality disorder.

Narcissistic Personality Disorder – What is It?

Narcissus is a term that comes from a character in Greek mythology. The myth tells how a man sees himself reflected in a pool of water and fall in love with the image he sees. An extreme sense of self-worth, prone to irritated for the slightest reason and are quick to anger. (Nordqvist, 2018)

Narcissism is a trait and actually, we all have some level of narcissism in our psychological makeup. This doesn't mean that all of us have a disorder but it does mean that we do have the trait, which is much different than the disorder.

We all tend to like to look our best; when we wake up and prepare for our day we shower, brush our teeth, comb or brush our hair, get it cut and styled, wear attractive clothing that are pleasing to the eye, keep ourselves in shape, put makeup on, etc., all the things that make us appear to be attractive to ourselves and others. There is a certain amount of vanity and self-love that we have for ourselves.

Feeling that way about ourselves is a normal way to feel. Wanting to look our best is not over-exaggerated or symptoms of self-importance. We all like to feel admired and it is a natural thing to feel good about ourselves and receive admiration from others. There may be times that we even want to call attention to our accomplishments. There's nothing wrong with doing that.

But if you have people say your demanding, manipulative, or lean towards exaggerated boastfulness, you may have a condition that's more serious than you realize.

Narcissistic Personality Disorder (NPD) is a psychological condition. It affects approximately one percent of the population, with primarily men being affected. This condition causes people who are afflicted to have a deep need for admiration and attention that is excessive, a sense of self that is highly inflated, show zero empathy for others, and have troubled relationships.

This disorder has those who are narcissists think they're better than everyone else and should be treated in a special manner. They are people who dole out condescension and insults at others and are highly insulted at the minutest of disagreements or the hint of criticism. (Smith, 2018)

In our celebrity-driven, selfie-obsessed world of today, the word narcissism is thrown out pretty frequently and usually describes a person who seems to be vain or totally full of themselves.

However, narcissism is not about self-love, in psychological terms. It is about people with narcissistic personality disorder are self-absorbed and in love with their spectacular image of themselves. The self-image is distorted. This disorder allows them to avoid their feelings of insecurity and that is why they are in love with their inflated self-image.

The emotions of a narcissist can be intense and unstable. They are excessively concerned with their power, prestige, personal adequacy, and vanity. There are displays of braggadocio and an elevated sense of superiority.

Many of the feelings a narcissist has are deep-rooted. They don't recognize that they are living in with a mental disorder. They think they are perfectly fine and it's everyone else who has a problem. For a narcissist, it takes a great amount of work to sustain the delusion of their majestic being. This is where the abnormal behaviors and flawed attitudes come in.

The narcissistic personality disorder is where people see their interests, their opinions and themselves as the only things that really matter. This is a characteristic of those who are egocentric NPD. (Nordqvist, 2018)

Other characteristics of a narcissist are they're demanding, arrogant, and manipulative ways. They also tend to be preoccupied with vanity, prestige, and power. These characteristics usually start early in adulthood and are consistently apparent in a number of different settings, such as in a relationship or their work environment.

People with NPD have such an elevated sense of self that they try to attach themselves with people they believe to be gifted or unique, thereby enhancing their own self-esteem. (Psychology Today, 2019)

There shouldn't be any confusion with a narcissistic personality disorder and high self-esteem or self-confidence. You can have high self-esteem and still remain humble. But a person with NPD is more likely to be selfish, ignore other people's feelings, and are boastful about their accomplishments.

As stated, the reason for this type of condition is to have a facade of high self-esteem, but in reality, it hides the feeling of insecurity. This concept is supported by the way these individuals get defensive when they are provoked.

A previous concept of NPD was that a person suffering from NPD had a tendency to have high self-esteem both as a facade and within their psyche. That is not the case.

Living with a person who has a narcissistic personality disorder negatively affects your everyday life. Living with this type of person is usually an unhappy one on the receiving end of this type of personality condition. You are not recognized for your own accomplishments. Your personal relationships and your work probably suffer.

People with a narcissistic personality disorder do not realize the negative and damaging effects their behavior is having on those around them, as well as on themselves. If you have this type of personality disorder, you will not have people who really like you or want to be around you.

Interestingly enough, there are people who are drawn to a person with a narcissistic personality disorder. You may be attracted to the type of self-confidence and excitement that is the aura that encompasses a person with NPD.

But, as time goes on and you get to know the person better and in depth, you may begin to be turned off by the same traits that are part of the destructive condition and that was what attracted you to that person in the first place. When you realize that many of the traits are not attractive anymore—their grandiosity of self, their unemotional interactions in relationships, their arrogance, insulting name-calling, and their lack of empathy for others, you will be turned off and want to distance yourself from them. (Gregory, 2019)

There are many concerns when dealing with a narcissistic personality disorder. Some have to do with dealing with the disorder on a personal level, like with a parent or spouse that can be very debilitating to the psyche and the spirit.

People with NPD think nothing of besmirching the reputation of others if it means that they can continue to look upon as they see themselves—someone without flaws. They will do anything to maintain that pretense.

Their sensitivities are extreme and illogical, at times associating the smallest observations with their fear of being seen as imperfect. They will do anything to meet their own self-absorbed "perfect" image and degrade, humiliate, and destroy anything or anyone who casts any doubts about that image.

However, the relationship with a person with NPD begins, it usually does not go well. This goes for any relationship. A parental, marriage, business relationship—they are all affected by narcissistic personality disorder.

Over time these relationships change both the person with the disorder and the person who is on the receiving end. What begins as an interesting and somewhat exciting relationship, as in a marriage, can end up having the person whose personality was once "perfect" begins to show their anger, their demanding and critical side of their personality.

Substance abuse, drugs and alcohol, and alcohol make the situation worse. Some people who suffer from NPD can be not only verbally abusive but physically abusive as well. It becomes even more complicated when the person that is being abused still loves the person who abuses them. (Skerritt, 2019)

The Difference Between Normal Narcissism and Narcissistic Personality Disorder

As previously stated, there is narcissism in all of us. It is to that extent that makes it a personality disorder. An example is taking selfies with your phone. Taking selfies during special events and fun times with family and friends is fine. Taking them daily and posting them for practically everything you do? Overboard.

It's understandable why the word narcissist is thrown around rather liberally because of social media and selfies. However, narcissism isn't something you have or don't. It is just like other personality traits, like empathy or kindness. These are traits that are on a spectrum.

One end is extremely gentle and kind while the other end is absolutely unkind. So it is with narcissism.

We all fall on to a point of various traits like kindness or narcissism. We all know someone who thinks they are more entitled than others or carry themselves in such a way that gives the impression they're more superior than others. Actually, some of the most successful people can credit their success and accomplishments in part to having narcissistic traits.

Highly successful people commonly have narcissistic traits and may have confidence in their abilities and accomplishments but again, this doesn't mean that they have a narcissistic personality disorder.

An example of a highly successful person could be the CEO of a corporation who has exhibited excellent leadership and abilities to run a major company. Being self-absorbed can provide that person the needed focus to perform well and succeed.

The extreme of narcissism is when the person's abilities are overestimated and displays an arrogance where they think themselves to be better than others and believe they have achieved more than they actually have.

Some people with NPD obsess that their life is perfect. They may have ideas that their relationships are where they live "happily every after" no matter what the real situation is.

Narcissists seem only to associate with others who feel they feel are almost but not quite, their equals. In their mind, no one is really their equal but there are those people who they will have affiliations with because of their position in society or of a talent they admire.

Narcissists need continual affirmation and admiration from people around them that they are talented, good-looking, talented or how well they do everything. They usually withdraw or throw a tantrum if they don't receive the admiration they think they deserve.

Those with NPD have no regard to the effect they have on others with their behavior. Narcissists are too busy focusing on how other people perceive them and really can't handle the idea that other people don't think they're as awesome as they believe they are.

Other people are exploited by narcissists to get what they want and think they deserve. They may develop a relationship and have an agenda for their own purposes. They think nothing of involving themselves with another person for status, money, or fame. And, they will either get what they want or, if they don't derive what they want from the relationship, have no problem dumping that person, ignoring the way the other person is made to feel.

People with NPD believe that they should be getting everything that they perceive to be theirs as well as everything that is yours. This means possessions, energy, time, resources or physical body are all subject to their wants and needs. They are people who drain people and use them with no regard whatsoever to the other person's well being. They use others to fill a never ending void within themselves.

Narcissists get in their own way when it comes to having empathy for others because they are so into themselves. It is difficult for them to realize and recognize the feelings or ideas of others as having any validity. They may not want to hurt others and usually have no idea that they have and they don't really care if they have.

There is deep-seated envy that is a characteristic of a person with NPD. Their insecurities make them feel they are not enough, don't think they are either powerful, attractive, or successful enough. When they meet or see another person who has these characteristics, this breeds envy in narcissists.

They will demean them, insult or humiliate them, and when called on their behavior, will just continue and say the other person is merely jealous of them. The narcissist does not want to own up to their shortcomings.

The following chapters will delve deeper into the causes, characteristics, signs, and symptoms of a person with NPD. Additionally, there are chapters on how to live with a person and deal with someone with NPD.

As you begin to read and familiarize yourself with the narcissistic personality disorder, you may discover how there have been people in your life that seem to have many of the characteristics of this personality disorder. Or you may recognize the traits outlined as some that you are dealing with yourself.

Hopefully, this book will be of help to either situation and to all.

Chapter 2: Causes of Narcissistic Personality Disorder

There have been debates as to how a person develops a narcissistic personality disorder. How does a person become a narcissist? Is it their nurturing, nature, or both?

Actually, there is no answer that is definitive in pinpointing how this personality disorder develops. It is possibly the combination of particular personality traits and external triggers. The narcissistic personality disorder is approximately up to six percent of the U.S. population. It is more common in men and its roots stem from childhood.

There is research that points to the suggestion that abuse, genetics, and other issues can contribute to narcissistic personality disorder can develop.

Genetics – Researchers are in the process of identifying some of the genetic factors that possibly factor in personality disorders.

Researchers study traits that can play a role in personality disorder linking fear, anxiety, and aggression to disorders.

Verbal abuse – Researchers studied parents who were asked if they were verbally abusive to their children, telling them they weren't loved or threatening to send them away as examples. The children who were recipients of this type of abuse were likely to develop borderline narcissistic, paranoid or obsessive-compulsive disorders. The likelihood was much higher than other children not subjected to verbal abuse. (American Psychological Association, 2019)

A natural part of development in children shows that most small children are selfish naturally and are taught how to "share" with others. The selfishness of a small child is a normal part of their development. They don't understand other people's desires and needs. They are only focused on their needs being met.

Imagine an infant in their crib when the begin to grab at their feet and focus on items in their crib. They are focused on their fingers and toes, stuffed toys and other objects that surround their immediate space. As they grow to be toddlers and interact with other children, they need to be taught to interact and share with others.

There are beliefs that the seeds of narcissism get planted early in childhood. Parents may form those tendencies in their children, either by being too indulgent by giving the child the feeling that they are entitled to anything they want and can do no wrong or treated severely causing an unhappy, insecure child and childhood experience. (Henry, 2019)

If the child is coddled by the parents, their receiving a failing grade, is not the child's fault but the fault of the teacher. By being too severe in their treatment of the child, expecting more than what the child may be incapable of doing, the child feels that nothing they do is ever enough to please their parents. This type of treatment may give the child the feeling that love is conditional.

Either of these treatments can carry over into adulthood, regardless of how far removed a person with NPD is from their childhood.

Factors of Early Childhood Risk to Develop NPD

- Parenting that is insensitive
- Parents who intensely focus on the physical appearance or a specific talent of their child due to their own issues with self-esteem
- Negligent or erratic care
- Criticism of the child that is excessive

- Abuse—psychological, verbal
- Expectations that are extremely high
- Trauma
- Over-sensitivity
- Gene abnormalities that affect the connection between behavior and the brain (American Psychological Association, 2019)

A child who has a parent or parents who are narcissistic are seen by their parents as extensions of themselves. They usually request that their children exhibit perfection or point out how the child lacks perfection, traumatizing the child with their demands and expectations.

As the child grows and is old enough, cleaning up after their messes and doing assigned chores is a normal part of teaching a child responsibility as they develop in their childhood. Some children who are not taught responsibilities and get away with doing chores grow up with a sense of entitlement because they expect others to do for them what they should be doing for themselves.

By the time a child is about seven years old, their personality starts to form. By adolescence, their personality and character have developed. At this point getting through at their formidable defenses becomes more difficult (Henry, 2019).

These defenses may result in an unhealthy acceptance of feeling disappointment by getting angry and throwing a childish tantrum. This is a way of hiding their insecurities. Rather than allowing this type of behavior, a parent needs to have a child experience a healthy dose of feeling disappointment.

When they learn how to deal with those feelings of disappointment, it will help to prepare them for the real world. Allowing them to fail in a place where they can feel safe and are loved is a way to help in confidence building in a healthy way.

A healthy, lasting sense of self-esteem is needed to be developed in children, especially as they grow into their adolescence. The teenage years are confusing and challenging for youngsters who still have self-centered issues as they navigate their way in this age group seeking their independence. (Johnson, 2017)

A healthy level of self-esteem means that a child has the belief that they are worthy and are loved by their family and in society. The usual self-centeredness of childhood needs to change to make way to adulthood. The teenager needs to grow and function with family members and society. They need to develop the ability to gain empathy for other people's pain and distress as well as other people's points of view.

A mental attitude that is healthy should eventually exhibit a sincere sign about the well-being of others. Those who do not develop empathy during the growth to adulthood is a sign that warns of the development of a serious personality disorder when reaching adulthood, including narcissism.

Child psychologists and clinicians are not eager to determine a diagnosis of a child under the age of 18 years with NPD. The feeling is that teens have a tendency to be self-centered naturally. It isn't unusual.

Children who are preteens can't manipulate because they're not developed enough to do so.

However, there may be one or more warning signs in a teenager that there is a possibility that leans towards narcissism. Some of the signs are:

- Making fun, degrading, or threatening people. This could include members of their family, along with their parents, and other adults on a continual basis.
- The need to win regardless of anyone getting hurt
- Lying to benefit themselves. They will even lie about their lying, accuse and blame others saying whatever happened is their fault, deflect accountability
- Their view of their self-worth is egotistical
- Having their needs met over everyone else
- Acting as if they deserve special treatment to get whatever they want because they feel entitled
- When criticized or upset they respond aggressively

- If a situation turns out badly, there is blame heaped on others even if they are the ones at fault
- They are excessively competitive than cooperative

If you sense that your child or one that you know has behavior patterns described above, focus on implementing the following:

- Put a stop to entitled actions and attitudes. Teach them that they are no better than others and should not act that way.
- Teach empathy.
- Show how being dominant, controlling, or tough are overshadowed by being kind and honest.
- Let the child know that they're acting in a selfish manner and that it is unacceptable. This puts a damper on any greed actions.
- Remind the child that actions speak louder than words and that other people should be thought of and put first. Don't allow them to turn their actions around by saying they are doing for others when they are really doing something for their own benefit.

- Disallow any false blame for their failures or problems. Teach them to take responsibility for their actions.

Help the child build self-esteem that is healthy and balanced. NPD can occur when a child has low self-esteem and uses NPD to support their ego

People with narcissistic personality disorder show a lack of empathy. This is shown by their words, not their actions. They react on the basis of how their egos are affected. This is how their information is filtered. The actions that are displayed reveal a grandiose belief of their own uniqueness and superiority. In addition, they also feel a need to be admired and worshipped (Johnson, 2017).

The resistance to feeling vulnerable at any time is one of the roots and cause of NPD. People with a narcissistic personality disorder do not trust anyone in relationships, especially in relationships that are close. This distrust of feeling close to others in relationships has them refusing to place themselves in a vulnerable position. The appearance of superiority and grandness is a façade and actually lives in a state of anxiety.

It's unnatural for a person to constantly feel great about themselves. However, narcissists try to feel that way, afraid to acknowledge weaknesses that will allow others to possibly have power over them or take advantage of them. Their way of handling this fear is to act more powerful and stronger than they actually feel. The root of the problem is the fear of feeling vulnerable. This is the main aversion in the psychological makeup of a narcissist (Johnson, 2017).

Although there is no distinct point to exactly when or how narcissistic personality disorder first forms in a person, it is believed that genetics, traumatic events, childhood abuse, and negative parenting all play a part in the disorders beginnings.

Chapter 3: Signs and Symptoms of the Narcissistic Personality Disorder and Their Traits

How are the signs, symptoms, and traits of a narcissistic personality disorder recognized? Do you suffer from the disorder or do you know someone who fits some of the traits already described in the previous chapters?

As was pointed out in Chapter 1, we all have narcissistic traits. To be a happy person living a healthy, fulfilled life, it is normal to possess a sense of uniqueness and importance. Taking pride in our appearance and what we accomplish in our business or personal life is signs of a narcissistic personality disorder. It is normal to have these types of feelings about ourselves.

The difference between a person with NPD and those who are normal in their assessment of who they are is not that the non-NPD person does not view who they are as all-consuming and taken to the extreme. We don't obsess over who we are and how the world views us and how everything should be about us. We don't surround ourselves with status symbols or only associate with persons of prestige.

The narcissistic personality disorder is about a self-image that's distorted, unstable, intense emotions, and extreme concerns with adequacy, prestige, vanity, and power. Add into this mix an exaggerated sense of superiority and lack of empathy.

They talk about themselves continually – People with NPD think and talk about themselves continuously. They talk about their achievements, their appearance, accomplishments, or talents. Their achievements are always better than all others and they exaggerate about how attractive they are. Their comments are usually extreme and usually not a true reflection of who they really are.

They also lack empathy, never considering how others are feeling or asking others how they're feeling or about their thoughts. They don't understand or really care about the feelings and needs of others. You may have a serious medical condition and talk to a person about it and before you know it they've changed the subject and are talking about their recent vacation (George, Katherine, 2018).

They love to fantasize – according to researchers, people with NPD are apt to have minds that are filled with exaggerated and elaborate fantasies about their power, beauty, success, or their perfect relationships. They feel entitled to have the best of everything. All the status symbols like clothing, cars, their home, even brag about the schools they attended or places they've been.

No one as anything better than them, or are smarter, or more attractive. These fantasies fend off their emptiness, avoid their feelings of insignificance and imperfection. They feel special and in control and if they do not achieve what they envision, they can become extremely angry and frustrated.

Their superior attitudes – As stated in Chapter 1, the narcissistic personality disorder produces people who have a sense of self-importance giving them a feeling of superiority over others. They surround themselves with other people who they believe are like them, who are "special" by way of money, position or talent. These are the people with NPD want to be associated with.

The need to be praised constantly – Individuals with NPD give the appearance of being outwardly confident but their insecurity and delicate self-esteem have them craving for constant admiration and approval. They want to be recognized and feel the need to having people praise them even without accomplishing anything that actually warrants praise or recognition.

Narcissists are also extremely sensitive to criticism of any kind. Any person or comment that highlights their deepest flaws or insecurities can be met with rage. The narcissist will divert the conversation into a different direction or just plain lie.

Their sense of entitlement – This characteristic is overwhelming. Narcissists have a sense of entitlement where they expect others to fulfill their requests and they feel they should get whatever they want with no questions asked. If they don't get what they want, they become angry and can even throw a tantrum much like a child.

People with NPD look at the world and feel it owes them. They look at other people and act as if they should be "serving" them and their needs. They act out when they don't get their way and their needs and demands are not met (George, Katherine, 2018).

Using others for their advantage – People are initially attracted to a narcissist because their personality exudes excitement and charisma and people initially find them attractive. Because of this attraction, people with NPD don't find it very difficult to have people do their bidding whenever they want it done.

Taking advantage of others when a narcissist's needs are not being met doesn't present a problem as far as they're concerned. They do it with little to no regard for the needs or feelings of others. Due to their un-empathetic behavior, narcissists usually have turbulent romantic relationships as well as friendships that are shore-lived.

Envy – A very common symptom of people with NPD is envy. They envy others for the slightest reasons. Their low self-esteem and need to have people see them as superior, narcissists see people who have things that they don't have as threats. It may be a car, more money than they have, position, even education, is the cause of envy by a person with NPD.

In order to combat their inner feelings of insecurity because of the perceived threat a person or thing may present, they tend to put it down with insults and acts to cause someone humiliation.

Individuals with NPD also believe that everyone is envious of them. Although they want to be envied, they will accuse those who they believe harbor those feelings about them and end the relationship (George, Katherine, 2018).

The center of attention – Narcissists LOVE being the center of attention. They need constant praise from their admirers to elevate and feed their low self-esteem. They feel superior to other people and desire attention all the time.

Narcissists feel compelled to talk about their exaggerated accomplishments and what they're doing or planning to do—they monopolize conversations, which are really monologues that's all about them.

There are two types of narcissism—vulnerable and grandiose. It is the narcissist who has the grandiose personality that desires all the attention and usually receives it by acting entitled, arrogant, and being outspoken.

Lack of empathy – Narcissists lack empathy. They do not have the ability to understand the perspective of others, cannot grasp the idea of their struggles and have the disinclination or inability to recognize the feelings and needs of others.

Narcissists can say something that is totally insensitive after having shown they could be reasonable. They could complain about how they're so annoyed about how their mother is to someone whose mother was just diagnosed with cancer.

The worst part of their insensitivity is that they don't believe they're being insensitive and offer no apology to those who may point out this flaw. If anything, the narcissist will become angry at having their flaw exposed.

They are insecure – People who suffer from NPD are extremely insecure which is the main reason they feel putting others down will inflate their ego and feed their sense of entitlement. The idea that a narcissist is insecure seems a strange thing to people who think they are charming and attractive.

The insecurity of a narcissist who is vulnerable comes from their questioning themselves whether or not they are really unique and special. They rely on affirmation from others to elevate their feelings of entitlement and greatness.

Narcissists have low self-esteem. Their drive is to prove themselves constantly. They don't just prove themselves to others as well as to themselves. This is afflicted fears and feelings of inferiority.

Their lack of self-esteem and insecurities have persons with NPD frequently "fish for compliments" from others by bragging and boasting about their achievements. In other words, they know very well how to compliment themselves while looking for compliments from others (Seltzer, 2013).

They can be defensive and self-righteous – Narcissists need an inordinate amount to protect their overblow but delicate egos. Their ever-attentive defense system is easily set off with little effort. For people with NPD, it's not only how they react to criticism but they react to **ANYTHING** done or said that they think is questioning their capabilities. This can activate their self-protective systems.

In their minds, people with NPD feel their survival is based on being justified and admitting they are wrong or have made a mistake and apologizing in extremely difficult for them.

React to opposing viewpoints with anger – Narcissists are not open to being exposed as "wrong" and express themselves with anger. Their anger is exhibited because they're feeling some humiliation or hurt that happened in their past and their anger is the consequence of these unwanted feelings.

They project traits and behaviors they themselves can't or don't accept in themselves – People with NPD are bound from deep within themselves to hide any weaknesses or flaws in their self-image. Because of this, they take any negative appraisal of themselves and redirect them on to others.

In other words, if a person with NPD is assessed as being wrong or bad or mean, their response is that "I'm not wrong (bad, mean); you are."

Their ambitions and goals – Normally, having an ambition or goal in your life is commendable but narcissists take their goals and ambitions to an extreme level. They're better than everyone, incredibly special, and set limitless ambitions and goals and fantasize about achieving more and better over all others.

Their fantasies are about how much wealthier and powerful they will become and how much better they will achieve their ambitions and goals than everyone else.

Their sense of superiority and entitlement is the reason that they will only socialize or speak to those they perceive have prestige and prominence. They will also fixate on status symbols, like the neighborhood they live in, the luxury car they drive, or the exclusive clubs they may belong to. They will deride and disparage those who they don't perceive to be on the same level or have the same kinds of "status symbols."

They can be charming – First impressions of beginning a relationship with a narcissist, whether a romantic one or one of friendship, begins with them being their most confident and charming, a pleasure to be around and get to know. However, it's the "get to know" part that's the tricky part because once you get to really know them, you most likely would like to "un-know" them.

The relationships eventually develop where the narcissist's behavior becomes aggressive, selfish, demeaning, and irritable. They like to be in positions of leadership and love the power that goes with that position. Once they attain this position, they will manipulate others to do their bidding to get what they want. If they don't get what they want, they throw a tantrum.

They are extremely competitive – In Chapter 2, you read about how teenagers who demonstrate NPD characteristics are usually self-centered and can be extremely competitive. If the teenager grows to adulthood and continues to build on their NPD characteristics, they continue to exhibit those symptoms.

Competitiveness is one of the common symptoms of narcissism. The person with NPD want to win at all costs, no matter what it takes. They are obsessed with winning and the person with a narcissistic personality disorder has no in between—there only winners and losers and they are not shy to point out others who they consider "losers" in order to elevate their superiority over someone else.

Their constant need to win negates any ability to praise or commend the success of someone else or are put into a vulnerable situation where they don't exhibit superiority over their opponent.

Grudges – The facade that narcissists exhibit as being extremely confident without a care of what others think about them is just that—a facade. In reality, they are sensitive to the extreme and really do care about upholding their "perfect, unflawed" image of themselves. They are not very happy when anyone insults them or shows their disapproval of the narcissist's behavior. They see these actions as "personal attacks" and hold spiteful grudges because of this.

The person with NPD will not let what they perceive as "attacks." If they feel slighted, they don't let it go or get over it.

They're not fans of criticism – For most of us, criticism is an acquired taste. We have had experiences where we've become frustrated over things turning out the way we didn't expect or was criticized and had a difficult time taking it from others. That is totally normal. We are only human.

However, the person with NPD to accept criticism and handle the idea they have flaws and are not perfect just doesn't happen. They are unable to cope with criticism and when things don't go their way will not admit they have any fault or they were wrong. Taking any form of criticism or constructive suggestions are impossible for them.

Narcissists react aggressively and defensively to failure or criticism. They cut the people off who are trying to be helpful and react with angry outbursts, yelling, or exhibiting aggressive behavior (George, Katherine, 2018).

One of the other aspects of their being reactive to criticism is that they feel it is inferred that they are being negatively evaluated for their performance or personality.

An example of this is being asked a question that they may not know or have the answer for which they feel is asked to expose a deficiency or vulnerability. If they can't answer they'll lie and change the subject or respond with an answer that has absolutely nothing with the question that was asked.

They have poor interpersonal relationships – Narcissists are not cognizant of where they end and others begin. In their minds, they regard other people as being in their "space" in order to serve their needs.

Narcissists put their needs first and regard other people as existing to cater to their personal needs without regard to the needs of those other people. This precludes that relationships with a narcissist usually ends because of a narcissist's lack of regard for others and lack of empathy.

People with narcissistic personality disorder have many shortcomings that they can't or won't recognize are harmful in their relationships with others. The underlying motivation for their behavior is insecurity which breeds the narcissist's fantasy of how great they are and their attitude of entitlement because of their elevated sense of self.

If these symptoms and signs are recognizable in yourself or others who you deal with, it may be time to rethink how it affects you.

Chapter 4: Different Types of Narcissists

Do you know your narcissistic types? Actually, there are few, aside from researchers, clinicians, psychologists and psychotherapists, who actually know all the types that there are. To the layman, a narcissist is, well......a narcissist is just who they are—a narcissist. Types really doesn't matter when you're dealing with one.

However, the type of narcissist does matter in how they express themselves and how to deal with them.

We now have read about their feelings of superiority over others and their entitlement feelings that they are owed special treatment. The fantasy world they live in believing they are the most successful and powerful over others. We also now know that it is their insecurities, and that, deep down, they have very fragile egos that they protect at all costs, up to and including lying. Their lack of empathy and how they take advantage of others and how they use people by taking advantage of them for their own needs rounds out the description that is a person with NPD.

However, narcissism exists in a range. People with NPD do not all fall into the same categories. There are three major types of narcissists, each with their individual mixture of traits. They have different ways in how they protect their delicate egos and one type may have the same motivation.

Interestingly, within the three types identified by researchers, there are sub-types that typify how the traits may be exhibited to others.

There is sometimes confusion among mental health professionals and researchers. There are different labels that are frequently used that describe the same type. Additionally, there are labels given to two categories that are unalike even when the same type or sub-type are being described.

With all these variations of types and sub-types of narcissists, it has become difficult to grasp the type of narcissist being referred to and understand them (Milstead, Ph.D., Kristen, 2018).

Three Types and Five Sub-Types

Narcissism has three major types of narcissists and five subtypes according to researchers. They are separately identified by means of different terminology by various researchers. They give descriptions as to how they are connected to one another.

Three Types Major of Narcissists

1. **Classic Narcissist**

Exhibitionist, Grandiose, or High-Functioning Narcissists – Most people think of these terms when they hear the word narcissist as "typical narcissists."

These are narcissists who seek attention, expect others to flatter and praise them, brag about their achievements, and have that entitlement attitude that feels they should receive special treatment. This type of narcissism is the most obvious type.

They see themselves as the most influential, most important person over all others. They want to make other people envious of them or elicit admiration by their boasting of their accomplishments.

This type of narcissist can be charming and have charisma. Their ambition may match the accomplishments they boast about and you may be pulled into their admiring sphere.

If the conversation turns its focus away from them to anyone else, they get bored. They don't like to share the spotlight with anyone else. They think they're the most important subject and rarely like sharing center stage with anyone else.

What's ironic is that while they're dying to be recognized and feel important, they perceive that they are superior to other people they come in contact with.

2. Malignant Narcissists

Toxic Narcissists – This is the type of narcissist that is highly exploitative and manipulative who have the type of traits that are not only antisocial but are frequently thought to be compared with psychopathic and sociopathic characteristics. This type of narcissist frequently has a cruel streak that separates them from the definitions of the other two major types classical and vulnerable.

The goal that is primary to them is to control and dominate and will lie, cheat, steal, and use aggression to achieve it and totally lack remorse for their actions. They may relish in the suffering of others.

3. Vulnerable Narcissists

Closet Narcissists, Fragile, or Compensatory – They feel superior to other people that they meet but are not happy with being in the spotlight. Actually, they loathe it. They usually like to be associated with people who they feel are special rather than getting special treatment for themselves. Ingratiating others through extreme generosity or seeking sympathy to attain attention and admiration they need to elevate their sense of self-worth (Milstead, Ph.D., Kristen, 2018).

Vulnerable narcissists can drain others emotionally. The reason for this is how sensitive they are in addition to how demanding they are emotionally. Their goal is to be seen by others as the perfect creatures that they are.

This type of narcissist is prone to becoming depressed because the fantasy life they feel they are entitled to doesn't match the life they are living.

Realize that there are misconceptions regarding mental illness and personality disorders. Some people threaten to hurt themselves or actually do because they are looking for attention. That being said, understand that Vulnerable narcissists are ones that threaten to do self-harm so they'll get attention. However, they rarely go through with the threat.

Vulnerable narcissists usually appear calm and introverted. However, because of the self-esteem issues that they deal with, the control of their emotions can still be difficult (Abby, 2018).

Five Sub-Types of Narcissists

Sub-Types 1 – Overt and Covert – Sub-Type 1 is described as in using methods to get their needs met are more upfront and public or more secretive and stealth.

Sub-types have characteristics that are related to the type of narcissist that they are. An example of this is an *Overt and Covert Sub-Types.* These sub-types may both insult a person who they perceive to be a threat because the person has a better pedigree than the narcissist. As we know, narcissists have a self-image that is far better than anyone else all the while protecting their fragile ego and insecurities.

Both of the Overt and Covert Sub-Types will put this person down, be boastful, and seek opportunities to use people to fulfill their needs. However, the Overt Narcissists will do so in a noticeable, public way, whereas the Covert Narcissists will be quieter and more passive-aggressive about it.

Overt Narcissists will be more out in the open about using manipulative methods to have their needs fulfilled. Covert narcissists will use more underhanded ways to be manipulative where a person on the receiving end of being manipulated is not quite sure if they were manipulated or not.

A possible example of an Overt Narcissist is a **Bully Narcissist**. This is a narcissist who builds themselves up by embarrassing and humiliating other people. They share traits that in common with the Grandiose Narcissist but they are cruel in the way they declare their superiority.

They frequently depend on disrespect and disdain in order to make others feel as if they are losers, elevating their ego and proving themselves to be a winner.

They will mock and belittle the other person and when they want something from the other person they may become threatening if their need isn't fulfilled.

Along the line of Covert Narcissists, the **Seductive Narcissist** can fall into this category. This type of narcissist covertly manipulates the other person by making them feel good about themselves. To get the other person to do their bidding, they compliment and admire them so that, over time, the other person begins to like and admire the narcissist.

The admiration treatment will continue until the other person is no longer of use to the narcissist at which point they'll ignore them and give them the cold shoulder (Burgo Ph.D., 2015).

The Overt Sub-Type will always apply to the Classic Narcissist while the Covert Sub-Type will apply to the Vulnerable Narcissist. The Malignant narcissist can be either the Overt or Covert sub-type (Milstead, Ph.D., Kristen, 2018).

Sub-Type 2 – Somatic and Cerebral – Sub-Type 2 is described by what primarily the narcissist values in themselves and others.

Neither of these sub-types wishes that their partner outshines them but they do want that they have someone around who boosts their status. To the narcissist, their partners are to be shown off to others as if they were objects added to a collection.

Somatic narcissists are absorbed with their external appearance, how youthful they look, the clothing they buy and wear, and how well their bodies look in those clothes. They can't pass a mirror without checking out their reflection and spend an inordinate amount of time at the gym.

Cerebral narcissists think they know it all and that they have stellar intelligence. They're always at the ready to give their opinion even when no one asks them for it. They know more than anyone in the room about any topic, no matter what the conversation is about.

They lecture rather than have conversations and are terrible listeners because they're busy thinking about their next sentence. They try impressing others with their positions of power and achievements. All three types of narcissists can be either of these two sub-types (Milstead, Ph.D., Kristen, 2018).

Sub-Type 3 – Inverted – Sub-Type 3 has been found by researchers to have a specific type of vulnerable, cover narcissist known as an **Inverted Narcissist**.

This is codependent sub-type. They feel that in order to feel special they need to attach themselves to other narcissists. They are only happy when they have relationships with other narcissists. They suffer from abandonment issues as a child and are also called victim-narcissists.

Narcissist, the term so often used in arbitrary ways, has made it hard to identify and taken sincerely and seriously, or to what group of people this term is applied.

Narcissists on a whole can be manipulative and exploitive. However, all narcissists are not alike and one type, in particular, that is extremely dangerous.

Malignant Narcissists seek to dominate others and can be abusive and destructive. They lack any conscience and actually find joy in the damage that they cause. Interacting with this type of narcissist can be harmful (Milstead, Ph.D., Kristen, 2018).

The Malignant Narcissist can be, by far, the most damaging. They tend to demonstrate a darker side to their self-centeredness, beyond just wanting primarily focus on themselves and be admired and held in extremely high regard by all who know them.

This narcissistic type wants to get their own way and doesn't care who they hurt in the process. They view the world in black and white and see others as their friend or their competition which in their mind equals foe. They don't care about the pain they cause others and they seek to win at all costs.

They may also have a sadistic streak as well as antisocial traits. Some behaviorists feel there is little difference between psychopaths and malignant narcissists.

There are other types of narcissists that fall into some of the aforementioned categories. They are not major but bear some of their characteristics.

Malignant Narcissistic Boss – This is a sad state of affairs for anyone who has this type of boss. Unfortunately, there are many in senior management and leaders whose personalities support narcissistic traits. Working under this type of narcissist can be hellish and for many, the only way to deal with it is to get another job if they can.

Research has shown that in leadership there is a darker underside and it frequently comes when power falls into the hands of a people who develop a desire for it.

There is a culture of "yes" staff frequently headed by management executives who impose their narcissism into the organization's culture.

Narcissism in the workplace is needed in some way because if an organization lacks it there is no leadership, no path to creativity and no self-esteem in the organization's culture.

However, a narcissism that turns into a personality disorder can manifest itself into malignant narcissists at the helm that often decimates organizations and then leave to move on to the next. The organization had become one of "yes" regardless of how it affected the organization's culture because the malignant narcissist did not want to hear anything but that.

There is no check on management and no reality check (Keogh, 2017).

Vindictive Narcissist – Can fall under the Malignant Narcissist. This narcissist will set out to destroy another person who challenges them.

If they are challenged (and the other person doesn't even realize what they've done) they will have an obsessive need to see the other declared the loser by going on a destructive rampage. The challenge can be the slightest and once provoked will stop at nothing to be destructive.

They will lie about the other person, talk trash to friends and family about them, possibly aim at getting them fired.

If this narcissist is an ex-spouse, they will have the other person in and out of court for the minutest thing just to be annoying (Burgo Ph.D., 2015).

The Role that Social Media Plays in Promoting Narcissism

In the last few years, social media has been examined and scrutinized for having a hand in creating narcissists. This is untrue. Social media has no role in *creating* narcissists but it does give those who are narcissists a platform.

Behaviorists in cyber-psychology are of the same opinion that narcissists can engage in social media because it is a platform that is ideal for a narcissist to gain the admiration and recognition they believe they deserve.

The types of narcissists noted in this chapter have been developed by researchers to not only declare that there is a narcissistic personality disorder but to show the major types and sub-types that exist and there are differences.

There are narcissists who are easily recognizable by many, like the Grandiose Type and Overt Sub-Type, but the more under the radar, Vulnerable Type and Covert Sub-Type are narcissistic types that many people do not think apply the word "narcissism."

Not everyone who exhibits traits that are narcissistic, it doesn't mean they are a classic narcissist. It's not as if they have NPD. However, even if they are not certifiable and fail the criteria to meet the diagnosis level, they can create a lot of damage to the traits that they do have.

Narcissists usually resist therapy and they're usually pretty happy. They are happier than people who have to deal with them because they're not the ones who have to deal with the negative impact of their disorder. It's the people who are impacted by them who are unfortunately on the receiving end.

You may be dating one, are married to one, or have a family member, friend or boss who are diagnosable narcissists. Hopefully, you have a clearer picture as to who they are and what types they may fall under.

The next chapter will cover how to live with a narcissist—what you can do to understand them, live with them and keep your own sanity.

Chapter 5: How to Live with a Narcissist

There is no way to sugarcoat it—living with a narcissist can be hell. Living with one is a lot of stress, unhappiness, and work.

People who live with a person with a narcissistic personality disorder may love the person, there are marriage and children involved, or their culture or religion may be the reason for them to stay with a person with NPD and they must do whatever they can to make the relationship successful.

Most people end up seeking psychological help to try and make a relationship as good as possible. Please read this sentence again if you are involved with a person with NPD. The operative phrase is "as good as possible." Unless you have a narcissist who is willing to cooperate with any type therapy to address their narcissistic disorder and the how it is affecting you, members of the family, friends and even co-workers, the best that's going to come of it is the relationship will be as good as possible.

If a person doesn't want to leave until they've tried everything possible to make it work, this is about the basic information that a person needs to know in order to handle a mate with narcissistic personality disorder while in a relationship with them.

Things will go a lot easier if you are in a relationship with a narcissist if you know three things:

- What it means being with a narcissist
- What is possible and what is not
- How to set your boundaries

What It Means Being a with Narcissist

The focus for a narcissist is on the enrichment of their self-esteem. They're narcissism can be thought of as a disorder as a self-esteem control where narcissists are continuously insecure about their significance, their importance, and their prestige.

Outwardly, they may appear to be confident but within there is always a doubt as to whether they are worthy. Their self-worth under the façade of confidence.

Essentially, the importance and enrichment of their self-esteem are more important than anyone and anything can ever be. That includes anyone they are involved with in a relationship.

When a narcissist's self-esteem takes a plunge, they have only two options:

- They fall into a depression. Their depression is one that is self-hating and the aura that is attached to that energy permeates into everything and everyone.

- They become grandiose, insisting they are perfect, invincible, and special and they do it at your and others' expense. They devalue other people around them in order to feel more important again.

Of course, their choice will be the second option and, as previously stated, the closest person to them, that would be you, will probably be devalued in order for them to feel their importance again.

They lack emotional empathy – Narcissists don't feel bad when you get hurt by them. They don't care and probably don't notice how you react to whatever is said or done that hurts you.

If you state that you've been hurt by them or complain they take no responsibility. They'll deny that what they've said or done is the reason you feel hurt. It's more likely your fault. You may have heard "You're too sensitive" quite often or they'll blame you for their having to say or act a certain way because you make them do it.

This means that, whether it is accidentally or purposely, your feelings will be repeatedly hurt by the narcissist. Prepare yourself because this is part of being in a relationship with a narcissist and it is inevitable that you will not escape their lack of empathy or hear an apology.

Narcissists lack the ability to realistically see other people and themselves – The ability to see both good and bad qualities of a person and being able to accept that both exist is "whole object relations" (Greenberg, 2017).

During early childhood, the ability to see both good and bad qualities of a person is developed by mimicking parents as well as a child being seen realistically and loved and accepted by their parents even with their imperfections.

If a person with NPD has the motivation and appropriate psychotherapy, this capability can be attained.

People with NPD who do not have "whole object relations" alternate between two views that are extreme of themselves and other people and they are either:

- Perfect, special, invincible and entitled (meaning all-good), or
- Flawed, unworth, defective garbage (meaning all-bad)

The narcissist doesn't have the ability to see you, their mate, in a stable and realistic manner. You, as well as anyone else, are either "special" or "worthless" and alternate back and forth between these two different views of you and others dependent on they way their feeling at the moment (Greenberg, 2017).

This is not based on anything you have done and has nothing to do with you.

When your relationship first began and it was in its fledgling stages, the narcissist was probably seeing you as flawless, special and perfect, the fantasy of being all-good.

As the relationship flourished and they began to get to know you, they see the imperfections (that we all have) and how you are different from their fantasy mate, they will alternate to looking at you as significantly flawed or all-bad.

There is only temporary happiness – The lack of "whole object relations" that the narcissist has will happen as time passes. This will affect the happiness quotient in the relationship and makes any happiness ever felt by the two of you fragile and temporary.

The feeling of happiness is sensitive to being unexpectedly upset due to the fact that narcissists are not able to sustain a positive, stable image of you, especially when they feel hurt, angry, dissatisfied or unfulfilled by you (Greenberg, 2017).

They lack "object constancy" – Fundamentally this means that it disconnects any positive connection between you and your narcissistic mate as soon as they feel something negative and all that is positive takes flight out the window.

Everything that you've ever done for them, the entire positive history you have with them is now decimated and out of their cognizance. You, in your confused state, wonder how this complete switch can happen. In one minute the feelings of total love, intimacy, and happiness are changed and in the next minute, your mate hates you.

The reason why this complete about-face happens is due to the lack of object constancy is a result of their lack of having whole object relations.

Realize if their lack of being able to view you and cannot concurrently see both your liked and disliked behaviors and traits and be accepting of you as a whole person, they only have the ability to alternate between loving and hating you.

These alternate feelings are based upon which one of your characteristic or behaviors, the ones they like or dislike, is in play at the moment.

An example of this type of switch is if you and your mate are enjoying a nice evening alone without the kids who are at their grandparents for the evening. You make dinner and plan on watching a movie together afterwards. It's a "date night" at home.

Dinner was great. The meal was delicious and you spend time talking about some future places the two of you want to see and take the family.

After dinner, you decide you want to clean up the kitchen before watching the movie so you won't have to think about it later. You let your mate know you'll be ready to watch the movie in a few minutes after you've finished in the kitchen.

Unbeknownst to you, your narcissistic mate is beginning to roll out their lack of constancy in their mind, thinking that your interrupting the evening by cleaning up the kitchen while they're ready to watch to the movie. Your mate becomes annoyed that they have to wait for you rather than you dropping everything and coming out to watch the movie.

You come out and sit on the couch, ready to watch the movie and continue enjoying your date night with your mate. However, by this time your mate is angry that you were so inconsiderate making them wait to watch the movie. They relate how your being inconsiderate and rude makes them think you don't care about them or, for that matter, love them or your time together.

You can't believe that this is the outcome of your doing the simplest of things— cleaning up the kitchen so you can enjoy the movie and not think about cleaning up afterwards. Being accused of being inconsiderate and not caring is, to you, beyond the pale when in actuality you have always been there for your mate.

If you are in a relationship with a narcissist, you already know the occurrence of this type of situation and how it's made you feel. If you're planning to be in a relationship with a narcissist, then you need to be aware and prepare for the type of situation that was just described. It's unavoidable and inevitable because you are a different person than you mate.

What this means is that you are different and have an immensely different set of feelings and sensitivities. What you may see behavior that is inoffensive may cause your narcissistic mate's insecurity to be triggered. All the warm and fuzzy feelings that you had momentarily shared disappear. The narcissistic mate is now angry and they begin devaluing you.

While your narcissistic mate is busy spewing their anger at you, you're in shock that their entire attitude and demeanor has taken a sudden 360° turn. Only a few minutes ago all was well but now an argument ensues with you defending yourself from false and ridiculously unfair accusations.

What is Possible and What is Not

Narcissists do not accept blame—ever!

They see themselves as either perfect or worthless and seldom, if ever, are willing to take responsibility for anything they do is wrong. Admitting that they are wrong and accepting responsibility or blame is, to them, admitting they are imperfect and worthless. If they do accept blame, their self-esteem is demolished and their self-hatred issues come into play. They also think that because they're "flawed" that you'll dislike them and that thought makes them feel worse.

Remember the argument over cleaning up the kitchen before watching the movie? Well, to continue, your narcissistic mate is in a better mood. They want to get close and say good morning with a hug, but you're not having it. You let your mate know that the evening was ruined because of the argument. They turn it around and blame you because you chose to clean up the kitchen instead of watching the movie first and making them wait. And with these vastly different viewpoints, the argument begins again.

Narcissists never apologize – Narcissists do not accept blame, as you now know, because for them it's too humiliating to do so. That being said, they probably won't offer an apology either, even if they know they're wrong. Don't expect any apology, at least not in verbally.

An equivalent to an apology for a narcissist is to offer sweet offerings like taking you out to your favorite restaurant or buying a present and surprising you. This is a reparative gesture that, if you want peace and the relationship to move forward from the argument, accept the gesture and drop the demand for an apology.

Pick which battles to fight – When you receive unintended, negligible insults, you need to learn to let them go. Telling your narcissistic mate each time they insult you and hurt your feelings, the relationship will eventually go sour finding you and your mate warring constantly.

The fights that should ensue, although it would be so much easier to discuss rather than to bicker, are those when intentional and serious insults are hurled at you and cross specific boundaries that you will defend by departing and ending the relationship.

If the boundaries that you set are disrespected by your narcissist and they refuse to acknowledge their culpability, be prepared to end and leave the relationship.

Remember, if you don't admonish your narcissist and let them get away with it, they will do and say anything they want if you allow them to do so.

Narcissists don't want to discuss and process pass arguments – If you decide you want to discuss your last argument, what went wrong and how to do it a better way the next time a disagreement comes about, your narcissist will refuse to even discuss it. They feel that you're pointing out their mistakes and feel you're just reminding them of their bad behavior and not really trying to work out your differences as a couple.

In order to try to be successful in working towards a better way to disagree, use the word "we" in discussing past behavior of both of you. Using the "you" word only inflamed and narcissistic thought process that you are against them and singling their actions out.

Defend the Boundaries You Have Decided to Set

Narcissists never notice or respect the boundaries of other people – If you don't decide to be clear and set the boundaries of the kind of behavior that is bad narcissistic behavior and draw the line of what they do and say is tolerable and what is intolerable, you narcissist will think nothing of saying and doing whatever they please without a second thought about respecting you or about your feelings.

Narcissists think nothing about openly criticizing your beliefs (if they're different than what they believe), your family, your clothing, your taste in movies and music—you name it—they'll go after it with insults and derogatory remarks. Many of their remarks and insults will be low blows in an argument. They will say disgusting and ugly things and then, later on, act as if there wasn't even an argument and nothing happened.

Creating humiliating public spectacles doesn't bother some narcissists – Public scenes that can leave you humiliated are nothing to some narcissists. This can be from loudly yelling and arguing and overtalking you on the street while you try to get a word in edgewise to leaving a busy restaurant because they don't like how slow it is taking for someone to take their order.

If a narcissist acts out in any of these manners once, they'll continue to do so again and again. This is how they perceive that their self-esteem is being insulted and the way they cope with that perception.

This is where you need to decide where to draw the line and set your boundaries. You need to make it clear that their behavior is unacceptable if they do whatever is the most intolerable acts in your perception. Be prepared to end the relationship if they continue to disrespect you and your boundaries.

Physical abuse may follow and escalate from verbal abuse – This is where your relationship with a narcissist should end. Unless you enjoy being struck and beaten, and do not draw any boundaries about the verbal abuse, your narcissistic mate heaps on you without pause, it would be a good idea to stop them from the very beginning.

It may begin somewhat inoffensively with a grabbing of the arm or a hurtful pinch but will escalate rather quickly if you don't set boundaries and state that physical abuse is a boundary where there is no excuse and a deal breaker in your relationship.

Relationships with narcissists, especially those between significant others, are never easy. However, if you want to stay in the relationship it will be a lot smoother if you educate yourself on how a narcissist thinks and reacts and what you can realistically expect.

Set your boundaries and stand firm to defend them. Draw the line with a narcissist and hopefully, you will be able to weather the storms that come with having a relationship with a person with NPD.

Chapter 6: Dealing with a Narcissist

Each of us has a tendency towards narcissism. There are degrees of narcissism, and the majority of people have normal levels of narcissism as a characteristic.

However, there are those who have very high levels of narcissism characteristics and you don't really know how high and how imbedded they are until you've become extremely involved in a relationship with them. You begin to notice that the qualities that were attractive and made you attracted to that person are narcissistic qualities that have become extremely annoying to you.

This person may be a parent, sibling or other family relatives who have a narcissistic personality. You have to put up with those personality traits but can't challenge or control. You may have an employer, co-worker, student, teacher or employee with narcissistic characteristics.

Although there are people who are narcissists, it doesn't mean that they're all bad. Some people who have elevated narcissistic characteristics can be charismatic, fun to have around, and excel in what they do. They may have the ability to lead your team to success at the office.

You may decide that the narcissist you're involved or dealing with may be the type that can be changed and you would like to help them through their change rather than ignoring them and limiting your interactions with them. There are some narcissists who fall in the "vulnerable" type of narcissist who you may believe will come to harm if you leave them by the wayside.

As you've already read, not all narcissists are alike. The way that you handle one that is in your life should be handled by which type you're involved with.

A **grandiose narcissist** believes in how great they are. In some cases, they just may be as good as they boast they are.

A **vulnerable narcissist** has a self-centered façade and being self-absorbed really hides a weak inner self.

Of course, either of these types may also have additional characteristics of what is known as **Machiavellianism** - *lack of remorse, lack of empathy and manipulativeness* (Whitbourne, 2014).

These personality characteristics are the ones that really annoy people. Their hostility and antagonism make them difficult to live with and they will practically always prevent you from achieving your goals.

The art of one-upmanship has been grasped by Machiavellian narcissists as they put their superiority on display while dismissing everyone else's opinions and feelings.

Falling for the Fantasy and why you shouldn't – Narcissists are charming and magnetic. They just sparkle and draw people into their sphere because they can with their attention-getting personality. They are really good at exhibiting terrific confidence. Getting caught up in their sphere can be easy. We think that they will bring about our desire to feel alive and more important. However, it's all make-believe and it's costly in the long run (Smith M. M., 2018).

They won't recognize or fulfill your needs – Realize that narcissists are looking for admirers, not partners. And, for your information, the admirer needs to show obedience. The only value you have to a person with NPD is someone who tells them how great they are to feed their ravenous ego. You, your feelings, and desires just don't count.

Check out how narcissists treat others – People with narcissistic personality disorder manipulate, lie, disrespect, and hurt others. If they do it to others, they'll do it to you and treat you just the same way and possibly worse because you are the closest person to them.

Don't even think that you're different and will not be treated in the same way. You're not special (nothing personal) and you will be treated the same way as others.

Focus on yourself – Focus on things that you want to achieve for yourself. If you have a talent you want to develop or changes you want to make in your life, this is the path you should follow. Create your reality instead of living in someone else's fantasy.

Don't wear rose-colored glasses – Stop looking at the narcissist in your life as who you want them to be and see them for who they really are. Their bad behavior and the hurt they are causing you shouldn't be excused or minimized. Don't live in denial.

Narcissists aren't open to change. To them, it's a sign of weakness and they don't want to appear to be weak; they want to appear superior to others. The real change needs to come when you question yourself on whether you want to live with this personality type indefinitely or want to make the changes that will salvage yourself (Smith M. M., 2018).

Set Boundaries that are Healthy and Firm – Mutual respect and caring for the other person's feelings are what healthy relationships are based on. However, if you're involved with a person with NPD, they are not capable of reciprocating these feelings in their relationships. It's not as if they're not willing to reciprocate, they're unable to. They don't recognize you, see you, or hear you. You are someone who exists outside of their own desires and needs. Your feelings, needs, and desires don't fit in. That being said, narcissists violate the boundaries of others on a regular basis. They not only violate boundaries but they also do it with a lack of empathy and an absolute sense of entitlement.

Narcissists don't think it's rude and invasive to borrow your possessions without even asking if they can go through your mail and your phone texts, arrive uninvited to your home, steal your ideas and let everyone think they thought of it, eavesdropping on conversations and volunteering advice and opinions that are unwanted. Some narcissists may think they're your brain and tell you how you think and feel.

Develop a plan – If you have a set of boundaries and have allowed others to violate them you won't find it easy to retain control. The way to have firmer boundaries is to consider what your goals are and any possible hindrances.

The questions you need to ask in order to develop your plan are what the most important changes you want and hope to accomplish? In the past, has there anything that has worked with the narcissist that actually worked? Is there anything that didn't work? How will your plan be impacted by questioning the balance of power between the two of you? When your new boundaries are set how will you enforce them?

When you are able to answer these questions realistically, they will help you make your evaluation of choices and the development of a plan a solid one that should work for you.

Unless you plan to keep a boundary, don't set it
– There may be boundaries that you have no problem setting and keeping while there are those that you've set in the past and then let it go and allow the narcissist to roll over it.

In setting your new boundaries, be prepared for the narcissist to not be too happy about them. They will test your mettle and limits in whether you'll stand firm by them or not. Let the narcissist know that along with the new boundaries there will be consequences and be specific in what they are. Backing down is not an option. If you do, you'll be sending a message that you don't need to be taken seriously and all your boundaries will be in jeopardy.

Prepare for other changes in your relationship –
You already know that the narcissist will not be too happy about your new boundaries. Actually, they'll feel upset and threatened by any attempts you make to have control of your life, with or without them.

Narcissists are used to having control over you and everyone else. They like to call the shots. They may step up demands in the relationship in other areas to make up for feeling they've lost control over you and the relationship as it was.

Taking a gentle approach – In some cases, there are those who choose not to give up on their narcissist and want to give it a try to preserve the relationship. If this is the case and it is important for you to do so, you need to learn to step lightly and softly. Pointing out their dysfunctional or hurtful actions and behavior, you're doing the worst thing you can do to a narcissist. You're destroying their self-image of themselves and their perfection.

When you let them know that what they've said or done has hurt your feelings, make an effort to give them the message in a respectful, calm, and gentle manner. Concentrate your message on how their behavior makes you feel instead of focusing on their intentions and motivations. They may do their usual routine of responding in their defensive and angry manner. Try to keep calm. If you see you can't continue the conversation, walk away and see if you can revisit it at a later time. (Smith M. M., 2018)

Try Not to Take Things Personally – Narcissists always deny their mistakes, shortcomings, and inferiority complex to protect themselves from feeling shame and inferior to others. One of the ways they accomplish this is to cast their own faults on others.

One of the most upsetting things to feel is to be accused of something that's not your fault or has negative traits that you do not possess applied to you as your personality characteristics. Try not to take it personally as difficult as it can be for you. Actually, it's not about you.

The narcissist's version of who you are is totally wrong – A narcissist's world is not one of reality and that includes how they view other people. Undermining the self-esteem of others is almost sport to them. Don't allow them to twist who you are and into someone you're not or thrust their blame game on you. Absolutely refuse to receive or accept any blame, criticism or undeserved responsibility. Those are negative vibes and accusations the narcissist can keep.

Don't bother to argue with a narcissist – Usually, when we argue with a person who is not a narcissist there is usually a back and forth and points made on both sides. The key here is that the other person acknowledges and hears you.

Not so with a narcissist. When you're being attacked by a narcissist your natural response is to defend yourself, try to argue rationally to prove to the narcissist that they are wrong. However, they don't hear you regardless of how rational your argument is. Arguing with them is a waste of breath. Just let the narcissist know you don't agree with evaluation and move one. Don't entertain the argument if they try to revive it. In order to control discontinuing the argument, let them know you are over and out.

Let the narcissist know that you know yourself – Having a strong sense of self is actually annoying to a narcissist. They see that if you have that sense of self their insults and projections of their personality traits and weaknesses on to you just won't work. When you know yourself, strengths and weaknesses, it much easier to ward off any of the insults and criticisms that are unfairly leveled against you.

Discard the need for approval – This goes hand in hand in knowing yourself. You need to draw your strength and approval of yourself from your own opinion and truths that you know about you. It's really imperative to detach and let go from the narcissist's opinion of you and any wish to appease or please them at your own expense.

This is a boundary that you not only put in place for the narcissist to abide by but one that you should promise to keep for your own self-respect and honor of who you really are.

Look Elsewhere for Support and Purpose – Let's get real about a relationship with a narcissist. If you decide to remain in a relationship with a narcissist you need to be honest with yourself. You need to fully understand what you can, and can't expect from them.

A narcissist isn't magically going to change into a person who will truly value you. That means you will need to seek out personal fulfillment and emotional support elsewhere.

Look for and feel what a healthy relationship is like – If you come from a family that is narcissistic, your sense of what a healthy, mutually respectful relationship is about. Because you've been surrounded by it, the dysfunctional, narcissistic pattern may feel familiar and comfortable to you.

Set reminders for yourself that as familiar as this pattern feels, it is also one that makes you feel bad. When you are involved in a relationship that is reciprocal, you will learn to feel listened to, respected, and free to totally be yourself.

Cultivate new friendships – There are some narcissists who want to control the people in their lives by isolating them. If this situation is one that you are in, you need to take the time to rebuild any friendships that fell away because of the isolation or begin to develop new relationships.

Spend time with people who reflect who you are – You need to spend time with people who know you and give validation to your feelings and thoughts. This will give you the ability to retain who you are and maintain t at perspective and avoid the distorted view that the narcissist tends to project on to you.

Seek meaning and purpose – Volunteer, develop a hobby, and look for meaningful activities. Make use of any talents you may have and contribute in a positive way to make yourself feel good instead of looking to the narcissist to make you feel good. Frankly, that's not really going to happen (Smith M. M., 2018).

What it All Means

Dealing with a narcissist takes a lot of thought, time, and patience. If you wish to continue to maintain a relationship with a person with NPD, the points in this chapter are to help you and be a guide.

Not all narcissists are terrible. Just realize that they are who they are and depending on what type of NPD you're dealing with, it will take a bit of a learning curve to understand who they are, how they think, and what their usual responses in situations will be.

As long as you can establish your boundaries, have a strong sense of self and friends and family who validate who you are and not who the narcissist says you are, you will be successful in maintaining your relationship with the narcissist and, even more importantly, with yourself.

Chapter 7: Victims of Narcissistic Abuse

The word abuse as defined in Merriam Webster's has three definitions: The first is a) to use wrongly, and b) to use excessively. The second is to treat cruelly or mistreat, and; the third is to attack in words and scold.

In researching the subject of victims of narcissistic abuse, that last two definitions fit into how a person with narcissistic personality disorder treat other people, especially those the closest to them.

There are many people who are victims of narcissistic abuse. It can begin in childhood with a parent or parents who are the culprits, cultivating a relationship, and marrying a person with NPD, or it could be a family member, a friend, a boss, or co-worker.

Living through the experience of being a victim of this type of abuse is incredibly difficult and sometimes, life threatening. It's almost like finding out you're in a relationship with a murderer. However, the murderer is not killing other people; they are trying to kill your spirit—your soul.

You have been dishonored mercilessly, lied to, manipulated, humiliated, and gaslighted into doubting what you believe and think you're imagining things. This isn't being inflicted by a stranger but someone you thought you knew. The life that you have is destroyed, shattered into millions of pieces.

You have a diminished sense of self, devalued, and eroded by the abuse of a person with NPD. You may have been stalked and bullied to remain with your abuser when you tried to make a break after the latest abuse cycle.

This latest cycle is set to abuse and kill your psyche and even your belief that you are safe. The abuse hasn't been physical—no scars to show for it but the internal scars from the wounds of the assault you have endured are there.

Narcissistic abuse by malignant narcissists can include psychological violence, emotional and verbal abuse, smear campaigns, a projection that is toxic and other forms of intimidation and control.

All this abuse is inflicted by a narcissist who lacks empathy, displays excessive entitlement and involves themselves in interpersonal mistreatment to satisfy their needs at the expense of others.

This may read as a bleak, dark world that you can't possibly understand how a person would allow someone to treat them so poorly. However, there are those people who live in this type of situation and probably at one time in their lives, they would have never imagined it happening to themselves to be caught in such a dark, dire circumstance. However, this is what narcissistic abuse looks like and it is real.

Narcissistic Abuse

Victims of chronic narcissistic abuse may have symptoms of Complex PTSD
(Post-Traumatic Stress Disorder) if they not only suffered in adulthood but have been abused by narcissistic parents. PTSD is also known as *Narcissistic Victim Syndrome.*

A victim suffering in the aftermath of narcissistic abuse includes anxiety, depression, a prevalent sense of worthlessness, humiliation, an all-encompassing toxic shame, and flashbacks that reverts the victim back to the memories of the incidents of abuse and the overwhelming feeling of helplessness.

When a person is in the middle of being in an abusive cycle, they can't really identify exactly what they are experiencing. Narcissistic abusers like to twist reality to fit their own needs, pour on the "love" after they dole out their abuse, and persuade their victims that they're the abuser.

If you, or someone you know, may be experiencing the symptoms that are outlined in this chapter. You or someone you know may have been in a noxious relationship with someone who has been nothing but disrespectful, mistreats you and invalidates you, or someone you know may be menaced and terrorized by a narcissistic, emotional predator (Arabi, 2017).

Dissociation as a mechanism to survive – You are physically or emotionally disassociated from your surroundings, have memory disturbances, consciousness, perceptions, and a sense of self.

The essence of trauma is dissociation. Experiences that are overwhelming become fragmented. Emotional numbing in the face of horrendous circumstances is a part of dissociation. You may escape from your current reality with mind-numbing activities, addictions, and repression because they give you an escape. You find ways to emotionally block out the pain and its impact so you don't have to deal with the horrific situation you are in.

Walking on eggshells – You are constantly monitoring what you say or do around your narcissistic abuser because you may say or do something that will bring about their anger, punishment, or you can become the object of their envy which will anger them further. Whether it's your mate, family member, boss or co-worker, you're watching what you say and do. It is very stressful.

Avoiding anything that makes you relive the trauma – Whether it's the activities, places, or events, this is a common symptom of trauma.

You still become the abuser's emotional punching bag because they feel entitled to do so. You're trying to watch what you say or do doesn't really work. You are constantly anxious about what you may do or say that will provoke your abuser.

Your behavior outside the abusive relationship will be affected as well. You may extend your hypervigilant behavior into other relationships and lose the ability to be assertive or spontaneous while traversing through the outside world. This will happen with people who bear a resemblance or are related to the abuse and your abuser (Arabi, 2017).

You please your abuser by sacrificing your own physical and emotional needs – There may have been a time where you were fun-loving, goal-driven, and full of life. You had dreams of who you wanted to be. In your abusive relationship, you are living to fulfill the agenda and needs of another person. *The narcissist's life rotates around them.* And that means that *your life revolves around them.*

Your friendships, goals, hobbies, and personal safety are all put aside to make sure your abuser feels "happy" and "satisfied" in the relationship. You'll realize rather quickly that they are never satisfied no matter what you do or don't do.

You begin to have health issues – While you're in the abusive relationship, you may have gained or lost a noticeable amount of weight or develop health issues that are serious in nature. You may also have physical symptoms of premature aging as well.

Chronic abuse can elevate your levels of cortisol (your body's main stress hormone) into overdrive. Your immune system is decimated, which leaves you open and vulnerable to disease and physical ailments. You have an inability to sleep or when you do, you have nightmares reliving the trauma you have experienced in the past with visual or emotional flashbacks. This can bring you to the site where the original wounds were inflicted.

You develop a mistrust – You become anxious and suspicious about the other people's intentions; every person represents a threat to you. You feel this way because you've experienced the venomous actions of a person you had believed in and once trusted. Your narcissistic abuser has worked hard to gaslight you and have you believed that your experiences are unfounded and lack validity. You have a difficult time trusting anyone. And the worst of it, you end up not trusting yourself either (Arabi, 2017).

You develop suicidal or self-harming tendencies – You are already suffering from anxiety and depression and you may also feel the need to self-harm or not wishing to go through another day and contemplate taking your life. You feel your situation is one that you can't escape even if you want to.

A "learned helplessness" gives you the feeling that you don't want to go on another day.] You may cause yourself to self-harm, like cutting yourself as a way to cope with your circumstance. Research has shown victims of this type of intimate partner violence are more likely to attempt suicide a numerous amount of time. This gives the abuser the ability to commit murder without leaving any evidence.

You isolate yourself – Abusers are known to isolate their victims, all the better to have total control over them. However, victims also isolate themselves. They are experiencing abuse that they feel ashamed to be experiencing.

Victims are subject to misconceptions about the psychological and emotional violence of victim-blaming. There is a trauma attached to this where victims may be retraumatized by family, law enforcement, and friends who may invalidate their impression of abuse.

The victim may fear there is no one who will believe or understand them. The victim withdraws from others to avoid retaliation from their abuser and judgement from others.

You make comparisons of yourself to others – A narcissistic abuser may have a penchant for creating love triangles or introducing another person to the dynamic of the relationship. This action further terrorizes the victim. What happens next is the victims of narcissistic abuse will feel they're not enough and internalize the fear they feel. They will constantly feel the need to "compete" for the attention and approval from the abuser.

Victims may look at others in healthier, happier relationships and compare themselves to them wondering why their abuser treats people who are total strangers with more respect than they treat the victim. The victim blames themselves and wonders why they are not treated well and what they are doing wrong. However, it's not the victim's "fault." The blame falls on the abuser—you do not responsibility in being abused (Arabi, 2017).

Self-Destruction and Self-Sabotage – Victims frequently brood over the abuse they've received and heard the voice of the abuser in their thoughts. This continual rumination amplifies the self-talk that is negative and can lead to self-sabotage. Victims are programmed and conditioned by malignant narcissists to self-destruct. This sometimes brings the victim to the point of suicide.

Victims carry toxic-shame and and punish themselves because of the narcissist's obvious and covert put-downs and verbal abuse. The narcissist has inserted a sense of worthlessness. The victim begins to feel they are undeserving of good things or be treated well.

You refrain from doing what you love to do – Malignant abusers are pathological predators. They usually harbor envy of their victims and their ability to succeed. The narcissist punishes the victim for their success. This punishing treatment conditions the victim to link the callous and cruel treatment with their interests, talent, and successes. The victim fears their success for fear they will be reprimanded or experience the narcissist's cruel reprisal.

Victims become depressed, have a lack of enthusiasm and confidence, and may step away from the spotlight because they fear to offend the narcissist. The victim paves the way for the abuser to steal their success over and over. The abuser undercuts your talents and gifts because they believe that you're second-rate or inferior; they are threatened by your talents and success. They fear they will lose the control they have over you (Arabi, 2017).

You protect your abuser – You minimize, rationalize, and deny being abused. These are mechanisms that help a victim survive in a relationship that is abusive and dispiriting. Victims of abuse persuade themselves that the abuser was set off because they provoked the abuse and that the abuser really isn't that bad.

Remember that the victim is trained to depend on their abuser for their survival. An intense "bond of trauma" is frequently formed between the abuser and their victim. Victims may even guard their abuser against legal penalties, give a portrayal of happy home life and relationship or share the blame of the abuse.

Narcissistic Abusive Language

Narcissists use abusive language in particular ways, with the specific aim to capture another person's mind and hold it captive. Narcissistic abuse is a term that should be preserved for the term *emotional manipulation* to avoid the risk of falling for a narcissist's tricks and tactics to hide, shifting blame and project on those they victimize.

People with NPD are experts of concealment and narcissistic abuse in forms of the specific use of language that is designed to manipulate and thought control that is all intended to emotionally manipulate another person into handing over their will and mind. The victim's thoughts and desires are stolen for the narcissist's personal gain.

Narcissists use language especially devised to have their victims question their sanity and keep them away from those who support them, such as their parents, family, and friends. The abuser's language instills mistrust in the victim of their supporters.

The abuser wants to have their victim believe that they are the only one who cares, giving the victim a sense of feeling abandoned. They promote the victim's feeling of worthlessness and make sure they're given no credit for anything they do, especially if the victim works hard towards accomplishing something.

Victims who fall prey to an abuser's ways and language doubt their ability to think and make their own decisions or if they do question if their decision is the right one.

The abuser also makes the victim disconnect from their own wants and needs so they will only focus on the abuser's wants and needs. The victim gives into whatever the narcissist desires all the while the abuser devalues the victim and their contributions to the relationship.

Victims ignore or make excuses for the cruel actions of a narcissist and obsess over their perceived faults or mistakes as if they are to blame why the abuser treats them so poorly.
The victim obsesses on how they can make the narcissist happy and idealize them. They do all they can to gain their abuser's favor.

Today, people with NPD have affected their methods on how to mentally devastate another person, usually a partner in a relationship as a couple. Their victim remains in an altered state of mind and body feeling helpless and powerless, at least until they come around and wake up to the true reality of their being abused.

One of the many ways a malignant narcissist prey on their victims is by "gaslighting," an erosion of your sense of reality. The victim exists in a mental fog, a twisted group of distortions that makes up their abusive relationship.

When narcissist gaslights their victim, they create crazy conversations and character assassinations. Your thoughts are challenged and the abuser invalidates your emotions, perceptions, thoughts, and sanity. When an abuser gaslights, it enables them to drive their victims to exhaustion so they don't have the energy to fight back. The victim begins to doubt their own thoughts or recollections of events.

The play *Gas Light,* originated in 1938 by Patrick Hamilton, has a manipulative husband drive his wife insane causing her to question and doubt what she's experienced. The play was turned into a script and made into the movie *Gaslight* in 1944 where the husband kills a famous opera singer and then stalks and marries her niece in order to find the jewels that he knew the singer had and killing the niece when he found them.

The husband gaslighted his wife, setting her up for situations where one minute she thinks everything between them is fine and the next he becomes cruel and accusatory of her actions making her doubt herself and question how did she provoke him.

Victims of chronic gaslighting suffer from a varied amount of side effects. These can include elevated anxiety levels, flashbacks, low sense of self-worth, and mental confusion. Cases of severe manipulation and gaslighting can possibly lead to suicide, self- sabotage and self-harm.

I've been abused by a narcissist – Realize that you are not alone. If you are in an abusive relationship of any kind, there are millions of people who have survived what you have experienced. This problem is worldwide.

Narcissistic abuse does not distinguish between and is not exclusive to gender, social class, culture, or religion. Your first step is to admit and become aware of how real your situation is and validate it, even if your abuser tries to convince you otherwise and gaslight you into believing that the abuse is not really happening (Arabi, 2017).

Echoism – This is a condition that arises from a trauma when a person is in a narcissistic abusive relationship. The narcissist may be a partner, sibling or parent. Echoists are people-pleasers to the extreme and are compassionate, emotionally intelligent and extremely sensitive.

Echoists fall into these victimized relationships with partners and friends who are really narcissistic because they themselves have a problem in expressing themselves and having a voice of their own.
People who are empathetic, emotionally sensitive, and compassionate can become echoists if they are oppressed and demoralized by narcissists in childhood. Echoists are fearful of being selfish, needy, or special.

Echoism is about pleasing people. Victims of this type of abuse are usually subjected to this type of abuse by a parent or parents. They also seek out narcissists who are abusive in their adult lives. As adults, they are alert to other people's emotions and facial expressions. They need to make sure the abuser is happy. Echoists are the emotional opposite of narcissists.

Seek help from a professional, especially one who specializes in narcissistic abuse. This will be your first step in understanding what's has happened to you and to help you break free and heal from this horrendous state of living.

Chapter 8: Stages of Recovery from a Narcissistic Abuse

Victims of narcissistic abuse describe their experience of spending time in a relationship with a narcissist as an emotional, intense, and vicious ride on a roller coaster. When a victim finally breaks away from their control and the grip they've had on their life, they believe the experience and wild "ride" would be over. Unfortunately, it doesn't end immediately and the victim finds that they're wrong in their assessment that it's over.

Recovering from a narcissistic abusive relationship is a process that takes time and has its ups and downs. It takes work, time, and conviction to succeed in putting the poisonous relationship behind you.

Feelings for the Ex

Regardless of everything your abuser had your experience, you can't just turn off the feelings for them like a light switch. This is true for a narcissistic ex because of the manipulation they used to cause strong emotional states in a victim.

When you left the relationship, it was a difficult struggle and took courage to do so. However, leaving the relationship did not squash the loving feelings you believe you still have. Staying away from the relationship is just as difficult because you are feeling lost, have a sense of loss and even grief.

The end of any relationship, regardless of what it is, is like a death and must be mourned. It is no more and there is a certain amount of recognition needed to believe and understand that the relationship is over.

You will fight the longing to pick up the phone and reawaken the feelings and reignite the flame that was the reason you were drawn into the relationship in the beginning. You'll have a desire to go back and work things out, even though you are quite aware that in reality, it's not going to happen in the fantasy way you envision.

This process of desiring to be with your ex again while you relive the cruel treatment you experienced can be painful. You are in conflict and feel confused in just the same way that you were in the relationship (A Conscious Rethink, 2019).

Your heart may feel that you are still loving the person who mercilessly abused you but your mind tells you that it's over, they abused you without a thought about what damage it did to you. You need to keep as far away as possible and never go back.

This is a dialogue that a person who has been subjected to narcissistic abuse and is in the process of trying to recover has with themselves. The dialogue that goes back and forth can go on for a long period of time and possibly will not be resolved.

There are two different views of the same situation. One view focuses on how everything was great between you and your abuser, and the other view concentrates on the reality of what the relationship was and how it turned out in the end.

There are things that you can do to break up this seesaw of emotions and speed up the healing process to end the stalemate and bring finality to the relationships where you have experienced abuse. Here are some that you can follow:

Write down all your beliefs about the relationship that are interfering with your being able to move on.

Here is an example of a victim's list:

- It was my fault I was so badly abused.
- I should have done more to make the situation work.
- They are treating their new love better than me. It must be because that person is better than me.

- I won't be able to find anyone who will make me feel special again.

This list is the emotional, *heart based* list that a victim will feel about ending a relationship with their abuser. The victim is wishing to have what they once had with their ex when the relationship was in a good period. This is the emotional side that feels the pain that they don't want to face or acknowledge.

The victim's relationship is over and they feel they will never have another relationship that will be a loving on and the "perfect" future with this man is over. This is their perception based on what the abuser has told them about their having any other relationship (Greenberg, https://www.psychologytoday.com/us/blog/how-do-i-heal-narcissistic-abuse, 2018).

The idea that wisdom is the only thing that can be saved from this relationship is too painful for the victim to face. The heart based explanation is attempting to convince the logical, thinking of the victim that there still may be a way for the relationship to work if they could have a do-over. It's unfortunate that this victim is still accepting a share of the blame that is more than they are responsible for in the failure of the relationship.

In your childhood, who determined that you always take the blame? – Victims who believe they are the person to blame for the relationship breaking up had a parent who inappropriately blamed them disproportionately. The victim takes more than their share of the blame for much of what happened in the relationship because of this treatment during their childhood.

This helps to understand that part of what is obscuring the current breakup in a realistic light is that it is a repeat of the recurring childhood blame situation.

Why do you protect your abuser? What does it get you? – Not only does the victim blame themselves out of habit. In order to be able to move forward and away from the abusive situation, it is a good thing for the victim to recognize what they derive from protecting their ex-abuser and applying all the blame on themselves.

Some victims think if they were at fault, they could make the relationship better. They have remembrances of how they felt at the beginning of the relationship—how special and confident they felt. No one else before this relationship made them feel as they did in the relationship with their abuser.

If a victim realized that their abuser is a narcissistic abuser and that they will never get the person or the relationship back to how it was in the beginning, then they have a better chance of getting on the road to recovery.

As a victim goes through the healing process and begins to see the relationship realistically and not through rose-covered glasses, they can write a true statement to the original statements they made at the beginning of their recovery.

These statements are what the victim's mind now believes are true:

- My abuser is to blame for being abusive. I am not to blame. My abuser has a history of being abusive.
- No matter what I could do, nothing I did could change how the relationship turned out.
- My abuser only treats the person well at the beginning of the relationship. This is how they lure the person into being attracted to them

They will eventually abuse the new person when the newness wears off and they have their next victim hooked.

There are many other men/women who find me to be special and attractive. They are attracted to me in a normal way and don't change into the opposite of who they present themselves to be

Whenever a former victim begins missing their ex-abuser or strays back to self-blame, they need to reread these statements again (Greenberg, https://www.psychologytoday.com/us/blog/understanding-narcissism/201710/the-survival-guide-living-narcissist, 2017).

Disconnecting from Family Members

There is nothing easy in the process of separating from members of your family who are either narcissists or who take the side of the narcissist in your family.

If your parent/parents are narcissistic it is rather challenging to distance yourself because they had a major hand in your upbringing, your past, and continuity and ushered you into the world. The bond you have with them may possibly not be a very strong one because of the narcissistic element in the relationship but as your parents, they will hold a place in your life and your heart.

Your separating from members of your family isn't always because they are the narcissists who abused you. Your narcissistic ex-abuser may continue to keep in contact with your family and may have them believe that you hold the blame for the breakup of the relationship. If there is still contact between your family and your ex, you'll have to let go of both for your own peace and sanity.

Regardless what the reasons for disconnecting with members of your family, it will challenging. Family birthdays, holidays, weddings, and funerals may come and go without your participation. Your own special events may happen without certain family members attending.

Your memories that are good and bad will come to mind every now and again. They will be packaged together with various emotions that can come to the surface and have their affect on you (A Conscious Rethink, 2019).

Isolation and Solitude

Narcissists are masters of isolating their victim and pushing important people away from you to gain and then, maintain control over you. Narcissistic abusers who are your partner will attempt to distance you from family and friends while family members who are the narcissists keep friends and love interests away.

When you've broken free from these relationships, you may face time alone a good deal of the time in the beginning. You may choose to be alone as you begin to rebuild and rediscover who you are and heal from your experience.

There may be times you do want to socialize but your past relationship may have damaged many of your good friendships that you could once count on or have affected relationships with family members who you were once close with.
Gaining your freedom can have healing and disheartening emotions equal in measure. This will continue to shift on that see-saw from one to the other for a time.

Wanting Revenge

A phase that you may go through over the course of recovery is the desire of seeking revenge and retribution on your narcissistic ex-abuser. You may want to have them suffer and feel as you felt while in the relationship with them.

Actually, this is a normal reaction because you are past your vulnerable state to your anger state. No matter how appealing revenge may sound and make you feel vengeance, what you really would be doing is opening old wounds. The stirring of unpleasant feelings and memories will only obstruct your moving forward on the path of being free of your past life and relationship.

Your emotions can't help feeling that your ex deserves a comeuppance but your moving forward and away from reopening your wounds is more important.

Your Curiosity

After leaving a narcissist, curiosity will be another reason why your emotions will be frazzled. You still have feelings for this person, even after all the negative experiences you had. You'll want to see who they're seeing, where they're going and what they're doing. In this day of social media, this makes it a very easy way to follow up on them and fall into that trap.

Seeing photos of this narcissist from your past can stimulate all kinds of emotional and conflicted feelings that will not do well in your attempts to rehabilitate yourself.

Narcissists have no empathy and don't really care how you're feeling. They have the ability to move on relatively quickly. Having knowledge of what they're doing can make you feel emotionally irrational and have a setback.

Realize that your wanting to have information and knowledge of this person is natural and understandable as it happens in the breakup of relationships under more normal circumstances (A Conscious Rethink, 2019).

Asking Yourself Questions

Why didn't you see the warning signs earlier in the relationship? Why didn't you see the red flags?

This is the time you need to spend asking yourself questions from yourself to yourself, specifically in a romantic relationship. You may take yourself to task and feel ridiculous that you couldn't see what was in plain sight. Now, in hindsight, you can see more clearly but that's not exactly how you view it.

You can swing on the pendulum of finding forgiveness within yourself to browbeating yourself. Each time this happens, you will feel upset and inner confusion and instability.

Another aspect of your path to rebuilding yourself is the question of trust. You will ask yourself if you will have the ability to trust again.

At the beginning of your restructuring, you will feel you'll never be able to commit to another person in a relationship again and envision a life alone. This feeling won't last forever. As you heal, grow and understand that you are a worthy person who people are attracted to, you'll begin to alter your feelings about trust.

You'll be more aware and attentive to any warning signs that will raise those red flags, but your trust level will eventually be elevated to a more normal level.

Zero Contact

You will need to do two things to bring the emotional roller coaster to a halt.

One of the only ways to really move on from a narcissistic abusive relationship and the narcissist is to completely shut down having any contact with them. Only when you've not only shut the door but bolted and locked it and cease having anything to do with them can you begin to heal from some of the pain and hurt you've endured.

The hardest time of your path to healing will be the first few weeks and months. However, as time goes on, the bumps in the road and the roller coaster ups and downs of your emotions will become much less until they are almost fully diminished.

You'll have those odd moments over time when you'll experience something that triggers an old emotion but these moments will be much less and farther between as the years go by (A Conscious Rethink, 2019).

Rebuilding Yourself and Your Life

You've had the narcissist in your past dismantle your sense of self. Now, you face the rebuilding process once you leave the past behind.

The rebuilding process, as well as the healing process, takes some time. It does raise the need for you to face your fears, your demons, and your anxiety. You need to face those demons and purge them. These are the remnants of the narcissist.

They are the wounds and scars as deep and hurtful as if you were cut with a knife. You now have to suture those wounds and heal those scars. They are all the beliefs about yourself that were false—that you were worthless, had no redeeming value, and were led to believe these falsities. The false beliefs that were developed out of your experience. These fallacies need to be dissipated before you can rebuild your new self.

Rebuilding yourself and your life is is not an easy road and there will be bumps along the way. Some days you'll feel like you're making progress and are upbeat about yourself and your new life. Yet, there will be days where you'll feel as if you're treading water and not making progress at all.

You'll have moments of exultation and confidence then quickly see it turn to misery and hopelessness. This journey back to self is like a roller coaster ride but if you hang on, you will see your way through, the bumps will become less and your elation and confident days will begin to outnumber your days of despair (A Conscious Rethink, 2019).

Healing from narcissistic abuse is difficult because, strangely enough, the victim only focuses on the good times of the relationship and tell themselves if they could have done things differently the relationship could have stood a chance. They imagine that their ex is showering someone else with the special love they crave.

These thoughts are normal at the beginning of the healing process. However, dwelling on this past abusive relationship for an inordinate length of time is unhealthy and needs to be dealt with.

The healing process, as we've noted, is a roller coaster of emotions. Do whatever you can to seek the help of a therapist who will guide you through the maze of emotions.

It takes repeated amounts of the cold reality to counteract the fantasy that was lost with what is now your true reality that is wonderful and irreplaceable.

Chapter 9: Narcissism in the Workplace

As you've been reading through this book, you've become very well informed as to what the characteristics of a person with narcissistic personality order are, some of the causes as to how NPD develops, how they can victimize people in relationships, and how you can deal with one.

Research shows that those with NPD believe they're superior to others, have little to no empathy or regard for another's feelings and that underneath this facade there is a delicate self-esteem that refutes even the slightest of criticisms.

In the workplace, a person with NPD is a co-worker who tends to be frustrating and annoying at the least. They can give you a pause when they realize you can pose a serious threat to their position or career.

Normal narcissism shouldn't be confused with a narcissistic personality disorder. Someone who likes to have a weekly manicure and pedicure or starts their day by going to the gym and drinking a protein shake afterwards to maintain an attractive physique. Those do not really qualify as NPD.

There are people who may exhibit some tendencies especially in competitive and high-pressure business situations but the pathological narcissists are found in the following personas:

An interrupter and hoarder of conversations – Most narcissists like to talk about their accomplishments, projects, or personal life constantly. They think that everyone is interested in their doings and what they're doing is more interesting than anyone else. Of course, there is absolutely little interest in other people's lives or a show of empathy. When you do express your opinions or talk a bit about yourself, the narcissist usually changes the focus back to themselves. They love the sound of their voice (Ni M.S.B.A., 2015).

They're name droppers – Hoarding conversations is not the only annoying habit of a workplace narcissist. Along with manipulating the conversation around themselves, there are narcissists who like to name drop. They also have a habit of status dropping.

They'll repeatedly remind people of the degrees they earned, the prominent school they attended, the celebrity names they know and mingle with, what significant projects they're working on, the praises they recently received from the head of the company—the list goes on and on and on. They need to continually make themselves appear important and have an exaggerated sense of themselves.

They love the spotlight – Narcissists love to be the center of attention. They dominate phone conferences, marketing meetings, client presentations—you name it, they're right there hogging the spotlight. And during all these functions that turn into the Narcissist Show, they like to remind everyone of their accomplishments, why their proposals and ideas should get special treatment. They like to keep the facade up of how powerful they are and their importance to the company (Ni M.S.B.A., 2015).

They steal ideas and take the credit – There are those narcissists who are famous around the office for swiping ideas and work from their co-workers. Then they'll claim a disproportionate amount of credit for the work or take total credit although they had little to no input into the project.

In situations involving teams working together, narcissists put in the least amount of work or is not a major participant to a project but will argue to have their name added to the list of contributors.

Another tactic of a narcissist is to go around and "chat up" members of the team about the project and then use their ideas to write up a project status report to upper management under their name alone. They don't even bother to copy other team members who, if questioned about certain aspects of the project, are clueless as to how management was informed of the project's status.

They "know it all" – Some narcissists who rise to levels of management not only take credit for other people's ideas (how do you think they got to management?) but they know everything about everything. How? Because they spoke to someone for five minutes, picked their brain, and made the information they derived from the conversation as their own.

This can be maddening, especially if it's you they're talking to and picking your brain. It's difficult to cut someone who exhibits this narcissistic trait, especially if they're your boss.

They may be charming, but do they follow through? – Not so surprising but narcissists make for charismatic salespeople, even when they're not working in sales. They are capable of turning on the charm and creating positive impressions. Of course, that's how it begins with a narcissist—they can charm birds from trees if they needed to in order to get what they want.

They can coax others to believe in the ideas they present and people who they feel will be beneficial to their cause will find themselves unwittingly manipulated by the narcissist so they can get what they want.

The problem for those who actually believe a narcissist is that they lack substance and their big ideas become missed deadlines, broken promises, overspent budgets, and complete failures.

Then, when the dust settles and there is blame to lay, the narcissist will turn it all around by pointing fingers at the actions of others that caused the failure. They couldn't have caused the failure because remember, they're too superior to have had a hand in that fiasco (Ni M.S.B.A., 2015).

Breaking the rules regardless of what they are – Narcissists think they're special, entitled, and beyond rules and regulations. They think nothing of taking advantage of people and inclined to take short cuts. They're entitled attitude includes handing in incomplete or false reports to management, creating business situations and schemes that are illegal and unethical, stealing office supplies and perpetrating deplorable white collar crimes.

These narcissists truly believe that anything they do, even if it is blatantly illegal, should be pardoned. They truly believe they should receive special treatment and are above the law regardless of what they've done.

Blaming others for their failures and averse to criticism – Pathological narcissists are extremely sensitive and averse to criticism. The narcissist's delicate sense of their flawless self is threatened by negative feedback, even when it is correct and justifiable. This can trigger their narcissistic injury.

Their usual reactions to being criticized are excuses, anger, and indifference that is pretended because they really do care about being criticized! That's the only thing they do care about and not about what they are being criticized about.

And let's not forget the masterful ability that narcissists have in turning the blame onto others for their own shortcomings. Someone else is always at fault and they make sure to let everyone who'll listen know about it.

Unable to relate to others – Many narcissists do not have the ability to relate to their co-workers as equals. They will either take a superior position and postulate that they're better than you in some way or will adopt an inferior stance and submit to you.

Both of these postures are premeditated to influence you to give them what they want. That is the purpose of any relationship to them. Their lack of humanity and empathy to positively interact and treat others as equals.

Passive-Aggressive traits – The passive-aggressive traits of a narcissist in the workplace are frequently done to put others down, elevate their own self-esteem and "superiority" and to get away with as much as they possibly can.

Their workplace behavior can include sarcasm, hostile joking that's veiled with a follow up of a *just kidding* remark, negative gossip, social and professional elimination, stonewalling, repudiating personal responsibility backstabbing, acting like a victim and premeditated acts of weakness to produce favor and sympathy from others.

Emotions that are toxic and negative – Workplace narcissists take pleasure in provoking and spreading negative emotions to get attention, keep you doubting yourself and off-balance, and ramp up their feelings of being powerful.

Any real or perceived inattentiveness or slights certainly upsets them. They are likely to throw a temper tantrum if others disagree with their views, or you fail to meet their expectancies.

Narcissists can be emotionally abusive by making others feel inferior to bolster their delicate egos. They are frequently ready to judge, ridicule and criticize. They don't like being imposed upon, and if unhappy with their work assignments, spread rumors about those in management they do not like or have had disagreements with (Ni M.S.B.A., 2015).

How to Deal with a Narcissist at Work

The Devil Wears Prada and *Swimming with Sharks* are two movies that exemplify working with a narcissist. All the tension, terror, cruelty and nervousness that these two movies display is, unfortunately for many, all too real and familiar.

It is a sad reality that many narcissists achieve top positions in management with no challenge, yet the path they've taken leaves a trail of relationships that are destroyed by their need to hold superior positions and executive status. The narcissist achieves their goals, but at the cost of broken relationships.

There is a way to work with a narcissist. One of the keys is not to point out their narcissism to everyone else. Even when the narcissist is proud and boastful of their behavior and is okay in pointing out their own possible flaws, it is never okay for someone else to point their flaws out and embarrass them. Doing this can be disadvantageous and harmful to your career.

The way to survive when you work with a narcissist rests with knowing yourself. Be mindful of your professional and personal assets which, for a narcissist, are viewed by them as competition. Also, be aware of any sensitivities and weaknesses that can be seen by a narcissist as a potential liability that they can use in attacking you later (Hammond, 2017).

Here are some guidelines to remember when dealing with an office narcissist:

- Keep your cool – No matter what the intimidations, gaslighting, verbal threats, twisting of the real truth or trying to project a guilt trip on you, remain calm, cool and collected. This could be thought of as a way to exercise self-control and you will be able to react more tactically when your emotions are lessened.

Since narcissists lack empathy or compassion, they can be ruthless in attacking anyone who they perceive as a threat. Someone who has healthy relationships with co-workers is a prime target. Realize that any form of attack form a narcissist is to undermine your standing to bolster their ego and perceived superiority. Remaining cool will also annoy the narcissist who is not used to being out-played.

- Take a moment before responding – Talk a breath and pause for a moment before reacting or responding to any demands the narcissist may make. A brief pause is effective as well. Narcissists like the immediacy of action or, in their minds, crisis to bully others to be on their side. Let your actions be seen as slow rather than making a decision that is forced or too quick.

- Disregard aggressiveness – Narcissists like to use a usual ploy by using body language that's aggressive because they don't have to say anything and let their posturing do the talking. They use tactics such as looking down on a person when they're speaking to them, leaning forward, puffing up their upper body or blocking a doorway in order to attain control.

- Ignore them. Don't call attention to it because it assures them that what they're doing is effective. Act casually and naturally. Don't allow them to intimidate you.

- Watch your body language – Some people have physical habits that give off signs of anxiety or nervousness like fidgeting, picking on their nails or skin, pulling on their hair or turning red. Narcissists often use the moments when their target is exhibiting these traits to strike harder. Remember that narcissists lack empathy or compassion so they use someone's nervousness against them and attack.

- Speak quietly – Every narcissist has an area that they feel insecure about and can be used to embarrass them when they need to have the line drawn on their behavior. So, in order to fend off attacks that narcissists like to instigate for their own purposes, do as Teddy Roosevelt, the 26th President of the United States proclaimed to "Speak softly and carry a big stick, you will go far."

- The big stick is for protection from those narcissistic attacks but it is a figurative, not a literal one (Hammond, 2017).

- Look out for their roller coaster of tactics – Narcissists use a pull in/push away approach that is, for them, a natural way of dealing with people. They praise and idealize a person and then follow it by devaluing them. Sometimes, they do both in the same sentence. Watch out for this type of tactic and reject the idea to agree with either so you can remain neutral.

- Set your boundaries – All of these points are important in how to deal with a narcissist in your workplace but this one has special importance as it is you who have to set the boundaries and you who has to enforce them.

In general, narcissists have no respect for boundaries. Initially, when boundaries are presented or declared to them by others, they take pride in ignoring them, showing no respect for them at all.

However, when a boundary is enforced consistently over and over again, they will eventually give in. There may be resistance in the beginning but keep your stance regarding your boundaries and stay firm. Over time they will acquiesce, and their behavior will get better (Hammond, 2017).

- One last thing about boundaries – continue to stand firm. No matter how a narcissist exhibits "good" behavior, they won't stop trying every once and a while.

- Attempt to bond with them – If you challenge a narcissist you will be instigating an attack against you. They are extremely sensitive and hate to be embarrassed and made to look bad. Rather than challenge them, try aligning yourself with them, partnering with them. This will be better received.

- Speak clearly and concisely – Communicating with a narcissist can be frustrating. A conversation with them seems to always be steered in other directions by them. Since there is work to be done and a brief period to relay instructions and communicate with them, you need to speak directly and clearly about what needs to be done. Be concise in discussing any goals or expectations.

- Don't entertain any of a narcissist's "what's in it for me" agenda.

- Devise an exit plan – If for any reason and at any time you feel unsafe when speaking with a narcissist, seek someone outside your department to speak to about your feelings. If you speak with co-workers the narcissist will turn any situation about your feeling unsafe about you being disloyal to the department.

- Co-workers aren't the only narcissists you may work with. There is also a dilemma if the narcissist is your boss (Hammond, 2017).

Dealing with a Narcissistic Boss

If you find that you have to work for a narcissistic boss, take a breath. In order to keep your sanity, keep a log about any demands they make on you so you can have a document that you compiled. Remember, you don't count; there is no loyalty from this type of boss so don't expect any.

Continue doing your job, if you can, if you have issues with your boss. Displaying anger or acting passive aggressively is not a solution. If you do, your boss will find a way to make you pay.

Narcissistic bosses are unable to inspire and have a penchant for undermining loyalty from people who work for them. In the end, it's a job.

Understand your boss as realistically as you possibly can. Give the job your best. Continue to work in the position if it works for you and if it doesn't, leave if they become impossible to work for (Banschick M.D., 2014).

Going to work and getting through each can be stressful enough without having to worry about dealing with a narcissistic co-worker or boss. Understand that it's not you or about you, it's about them. If you can work with this type of personality and have little to no problems, then you're lucky. However, if not, it's time to look for another   job.

Chapter 10: Regain Control from a Narcissist

There is a tale of Narcissus in Greek mythology who was the son of Cephissus, the Greek river god and Liriope, a nymph. Handsome, young and gifted, Narcissus had the potential of a full life. However, Narcissus saw his reflection that was reflected in a pool of water and fell in love with his image. He remained entranced by his reflection and wasted away staring at himself until he died.

This story is where the term narcissism is derived. Although the story is one of mythology, it's no myth that narcissists exist and they're not that great to be involved with in a relationship.

Most people who end up in a relationship, especially in a romantic one, with a narcissist usually have a difficult time dealing with them because of their lack of empathy and compassion.

In most relationships with a narcissist, it's all about them and their needs. A relationship can also be about narcissistic abuse which is extremely destructive and emotionally traumatizing. The abuse can lead to low self-esteem, attachment issues, and PTSD (Meridian Counseling, 2019).

As was stated in Chapter 2, narcissism can develop in childhood where an early trauma affects the child due to a neglectful or selfish (possibly narcissistic) parent or caregiver. To survive their childhood, they create a "false self" to defend and protect themselves against rejection and emotional pain.

This causes the child to grow into adulthood and create a façade to hide their internal strife, insecurity, and vulnerable ego.

How to Control a Narcissist

If you've are in a romantic relationship with a narcissist and are holding out hope that it will have a happy ending, you may or may not get your wish. It all depends on how you handle how things work out.

We know that narcissists love to thrive on power and control. Turning things around and gaining control over a narcissist isn't the easiest task in the world. It would seem that herding cats would be easier.

However, there are ways to get around a narcissist and get on their good side to disperse any sense of defensiveness the narcissist may have when they're dealing with you. Then, you can begin to use numerous techniques when you're interacting with them to coax them to get them to do things your way.

The one thing you need to remember is to control your temper to avoid the narcissist from controlling it for you (Wikihow, M, 2019).

Get on their good side. Listen to them A LOT – Narcissists need to be the center of attention and usually dominate every conversation they have. Actually, it's more of a dialogue with an audience listening to them.

You just can't "hear" what they're saying, you need to really show that you're actively listening also.

You can't just smile and nod and feign interest in what the narcissist is saying. If you really want to win favor with a narcissist you need to react to things they say in a way that displays how much attention you're paying to what they're saying

Watch how the narcissists react. If you're engagement with them is not to their liking, they'll let you know about it in a short period of time.

Offer praise – Narcissists think they're terrific regardless of whether you tell them or not. This is their exaggerated view of themselves. However, it doesn't mean that they don't like being complimented by others. When you're offering your praise, make is sound as genuine as possible.

If you praise the narcissist in front of others, you'll be racking up the bonus points. The more attention they get, the more they are pleased and they will be wanting to spend time with you.

The praise you give the narcissist needs to be genuine or you'll create a bigger nuisance than before. Narcissists will do almost anything to be admired and noticed. If you repeatedly praise them for a certain behavior, they'll most likely repeat the behavior again. Make sure it's one that everyone can bear.

You're not going to make their personality disorder any worse than it already is. Narcissists usually develop their personality disorder at a young age and praise you offer will not over-inflate their ego since their ego is already self-inflated by the narcissist (Wikihow, M, 2019).

Use language that is non-accusatory. Use the "I" word – Every so often you will have a dispute with the narcissist in your life. In all likelihood, they will feel affronted if you are verbally critical of them. If you bluntly criticize them, realize you will not be gaining a fan. Even though that's how the narcissist will react, that doesn't mean you have to bite your tongue and back away.

When the narcissist has done wrong and you want to point it out it can be simply phrased as an opinion that is subjective instead of being accusatory.

The "I" language diminishes the aggressiveness, defensiveness, and rage that the narcissist goes to in order to protect their fragile ego. Narcissists are known to exhibit these traits in excess, so using "I" will give you meaningful leverage.

An example of this can be "I feel hurt by what you said" rather than saying, "You said something that was uncaring and cruel."

Acknowledge concerns but don't accept blame – Address the concern by naming it specifically when the narcissist becomes upset with you. Explain you have a different opinion on the concern rather than accepting blame.

As an example, a report at work where some figures in the report don't add up. Instead of saying "You were supposed to double check the report and all the figures. This is your fault." Probably, in true narcissistic style, they'll think it's your fault and turn the blame on to you. You need to respond by saying "you may think I'm the one at fault, but that's not how I see it. I'm not comfortable taking the blame."

Getting the Narcissist to do Things Differently

Conceal your set boundaries as compliments – You know that the narcissist is going to act out in behavior you dislike. When they do, let them know that a positive quality of their personality would be viewed by others so much better if they remedied the negative behavior. The key to their changing and your boundary respected is to emphasize the positive quality over their negative behavior.

Your personal space is something that narcissists usually cross without a second thought or their even recognizing that they're doing it or that it's wrong. This comes from their lack of empathy, respecting the space of others and that others exist to serve them.

As an example, instead of saying things such as "Leave me alone! I'm really busy right now!" You can say this instead "I really appreciate the interesting story you were telling me earlier today. I'm really anxious to hear the rest of it but it would be much better if you stop by my office later this afternoon after I complete this project rather than in the middle of the day when I'm working against a deadline."

Concentrate on solutions – If you've made a decision and need to tell the narcissist that it's recently been made, the emphasis should be on the solution to the problem that you've made a decision on and very little emphasis on the problem itself.

Narcissists usually like to gain control and likely go back over the problem to insert their own solutions. In order to prevent any disagreement and save time, you need to halt the narcissist from focusing on the problem.

This principle can also be applied when you have only likely solutions instead of one decided solution. Present the possible solutions to the narcissist only explaining the problem they deal with afterward.

Side-step direct challenges – Narcissists don't deal well with direct challenges. They will probably perceive it as a threat to their authority. When you challenge their sense of authority the narcissist will stubbornly cling to it more than ever before.

If you say things like "Let's not see the movie you want to see" be prepared for a fight to ensue. Avoid challenging the narcissist. When it's not possible, present your challenge as subtle as you can to prevent them from getting defensive.

The blame game – just don't play it – A situation may be the narcissist's fault, but when it is their fault don't point your finger at them AND don't allow them to point fingers at you. Cut off any blame discussion by turning the narcissist's attention to another topic. The narcissist's ego (fragile, delicate, remember) won't let you imply that they are the guilty party. Avoid that discussion altogether.

The earlier example of the report figures being incorrect was because the narcissist didn't check them. The narcissist will probably try to push the blame on you since they will not accept blame.

After you defend your belief that you're not to blame and felt uncomfortable accepting it, steer the conversation by pointing out that the more important thing is to correct the error. This will cut off the blame game and you can move on.

Persuade the narcissist that they will benefit – In order to convince narcissists to make a choice for a particular course of action, the easiest way to do this is to propose that it will be a benefit to them. Everything that is of self-interest is how the narcissist mind views anything good for them.

Zero in on what the narcissist's proudest qualities are and appeal to that quality to make this more effective. As an example, the narcissist may be pretty pleased about them being clever and you need to influence them in accepting a certain policy at work.

Talk to them about other intelligent people who made decisions that were similar to another company and they were successful. Then mention other companies that did not accept the changes and, as a result, were foolish not to do. With this in mind, the narcissist will view that accepting the policy change was a great demonstration of their highly superior intelligence.

More options for the narcissist – Narcissists always have the need to have a sense of control. In order to let them think that they have control and power over any decision making process, ask the narcissist which option they would prefer instead of telling the narcissist they have to do something.

As an example, saying something like "We're going to dinner this Saturday evening at 7 pm" ask them "What time would you like to leave for dinner Saturday evening?"

Let the narcissist get the credit – A narcissist likes to take the credit for a solution, even if someone else came up with the solution. This is annoying, especially for the person who had the credit stolen by the narcissist. However, letting the narcissist take credit is something you should do when possible.

This is an effective way to persuade a narcissist to things your way by letting them think that things are being done the narcissist's way.

You may believe that you would be losing credit or prestige with someone like your supervisor. When it's possible, talk to them privately about the way the solution really came about.

Initially, you might have other people think that you're not pulling your weight or contributing to a project while the narcissist is taking the credit. However, that will change as more people in your professional or social group get to know the narcissist much better. Over time, they'll begin to see reality.

When they do, they will understand that the narcissist isn't responsible for half the things they claim to have accomplished. When this reality sets in among your group, most will learn that you are the one who arrived at the solution, not the narcissist.

Keep your cool – Dealing with a narcissist can be irritating and that is probably an understatement for anyone who's been dealing with one for a while. As difficult as they can be, realize that their behavior is not a reflection on you. The narcissist doesn't have a filter and behaves in the same egotistical, selfish way with everyone. It's not about you, it really is about them and their need to feel superior and entitled over others.

There are exceptions and boundaries, however. One particular person may have the narcissist on who they focus their attention. The narcissist may be treated the same as any other person would be treated but it might be worse than someone who is just an acquaintance.

When the narcissist shows behavior that is destructive instead of just exhibiting ones that are just annoying, begin to worry about remaining the way you're being treated and protect yourself from any harm.

This is especially true of a romantic relationship you may have with the narcissist. Any behavior that is cruel and abusive and you feel that it is escalating a bit more each time is pause for concern. Seek help from family, friends, or professionals to break that abusive cycle.

Make fewer demands and lower any expectations you may have – Understand that a narcissist is incapable of giving you any source of support emotionally or have a civilized argument.

Narcissists are in the habits they have had since childhood and they don't give it a thought in changing their ways. Controlling a narcissist can happen occasionally but you'll never change them or see those habits completely break.

It is frequently advised not to become involved in a romantic relationship with a narcissist. Prepare to be critiqued if you make your feelings known to a narcissist, especially if their feelings don't match yours.

Envision situations – Take a step back when you have frustrating situations with the narcissist. Visualize the circumstances from an objective, external viewpoint. Rather than getting emotionally stressed, question what you would advise someone else in your position. This will give you the ability to keep control over your emotions and from becoming overwhelmed.

Don't become too involved and concentrate on the person – Narcissists are human beings with strengths and weaknesses just like everyone else. However, realize that the weaknesses of the narcissist are quite obvious and if you've been dealing with one over any lengthy period of time, you may feel they are an enemy with no redeeming value. Although their words and actions have had a negative effect on you, understand that they have positive characteristics as well.

It's advised that you keep your distance emotionally and not become too attached with the narcissists in your life. Appreciate their strengths and sympathize their weaknesses but think twice about becoming too intimate. You may think you can "change" their narcissism, but you'll find out it simply will not happen.

Sympathize the narcissist and their narcissism because it is emotionally unhealthy. The person who suffers from this personality condition is actually being denied the full value of having human feelings. However, don't allow the narcissist to see you sympathize them because they'll probably feel insulted and misunderstand your feelings.

Breathe and stay calm – Remain calm and take a deep breath when you're dealing with a narcissist. The narcissist will always try to have control over you. However, if you keep control over yourself, you may be able to shift the outcome of some of your encounters with them to your favor (Wikihow, M, 2019).

Chapter 11: Overcoming Narcissistic Tendencies

Researchers define narcissistic personality disorder as a mental disorder. Those who suffer from this disorder have a need for admiration that is deep-seated and their belief that they're superior to others emanates from their extremely fragile self-esteem and their inability to accept even the slightest criticism.

Many narcissists are virtually unmindful to their negative and their behavior patterns that are frequently self-destructive.

There are negative outcomes to their chronic narcissism. These outcomes may include:

- Isolation and solitude with few close, healthy, lasting relationships
- Estrangement from family and/or family members
- People who have been lied to are used to be manipulated, disappointed, invalidated, ignored, invalidated, ripped-off, exploited, or betrayed cut off their relationship with the narcissist.
- Narcissists miss out on opportunities because of their lack of correctness or substance
- Career, legal, or financial problems from their inability to follow rules, their lack of accepting responsibility, careless extravagances or other lack of discretions. Their professional and/or personal reputation damaged by their actions or inaction
- Narcissists who do have a level of self-awareness of their shortcomings and weaknesses has an ability to free themselves from the delusion of falsehood and start the process of inner healing.
- Narcissists who truly want to address their negative narcissistic personality traits should

confer with a qualified professional who specializes in mental health disorders.

- Along with conferring with a qualified professional, there are ways for a narcissist to attain a better and truer sense of self versus their imagined sense of self (Ni, 2014).

What do you want to change? – It is important that you are the one who makes the choice on which issues you want to work on. There may be people around you who wish you would do certain things differently and may be suggesting those issues they think are important but the changes you want to make you have to do for yourself, not anyone else. If you want to be successful in this process, you need to start with something you care about. The issue you want to work on is the behavior that you feel impacts you negatively. Working on the issue you've chosen will keep you motivated (Greenberg, https://www.psychologytoday.com/us/blog/understanding-narcissism/201802/7-steps-changing-your-narcissistic-responses, 2018).

What triggers the behavior you want to change?
– Situations, behaviors, or words are *triggers* that bring about feelings of negativity in you. People that have narcissistic issues usually overreact when they're triggered and will do things they regret later on.

An example of this is Laura had a habit of angrily screaming when things didn't go her way. When she was triggered, she loudly yelled about whatever triggered her anger, publicly devalued the person she felt was responsible.

Laura wanted to stop yelling and devaluing people in public and later feeling terrible and embarrassed for having had the tantrum. Some of the common triggers Laura experienced were:

- Waiting to be seated at a restaurant when she had a reservation
- Going shopping at her favorite department store and berating a salesperson, who she felt was beneath her, did not immediately help her with a

request to find a piece of merchandise on the sales floor

- Feeling ignored
- A co-worker correcting her in front of their manager about a piece of information being added to a department report made Laura feel inadequate

Buy a small notebook and write down the list of what your triggers are. Begin identifying the circumstances when you are most likely to get triggered. Write those down as well.

Make a list of the behaviors you engage in while you are triggered that you want to change. Identify those behaviors, such as yelling at your spouse in pubic, or becoming impatient and berating a salesperson while shopping and becoming angry at your co-worker (Greenberg, https://www.psychologytoday.com/us/blog/understanding-narcissism/201802/7-steps-changing-your-narcissistic-responses, 2018).

After you write down all the behaviors you want to change, envision how you would ideally like to react instead of how you've been reacting and acting out.

Write those visions down.

- Laura wanted to take a breath and take a pause to think about the situation before she spoke.
- She wanted to stop making scenes in public.
- She decided that she would speak civilly and calmly to sales staff when shopping and not demean them because they're delayed in waiting on her.
- She wanted to understand that her co-worker was not trying to insult her in front of her supervisor. She realized that she had spoken incorrectly because she had not read through the report before speaking with their manager

Delay unwanted behaviors – Practice delaying your *normal response* when you are triggered. Of course, your normal response is the unwanted, unhinged ones that you do instantly. It is a habit that is wired into your brain and it can appear very quickly.

Here are ways to delay your response and keep calm:

- Count to 25 before reacting or responding (counting to 10 is not long enough for the number of years you've been responding in an unwanted way)
- Breathe! Take slow, deep, calming breaths. Envision a beautiful scene, beach, a beautiful vision while you breathe to relax
- Remember the last time you acted in the way you want to change. Take time to see what you looked like and how you acted and remember it so you can change it and rewire your brain

Substitute new responses – When you delay or inhibit your old responses to your trigger, replace and with a new response. Every time that you are able to delay the old response and use the new one instead, put a checkmark next to the behavior on your list. This will indicate that you've been successful in changing their behavior you've wanted to change.

Review successes and the areas that need improvement – Take some time at a time that is convenient and right for you. This could be either at the end of each day or once a week to review your successes and the areas that still need work.

Your brain is being rewritten. It takes time. Patience and being gentle and kind to yourself is important. The changes won't happen overnight. Continue to practice the methods that are suggested to work on the issues you want to change. If you stick to the program and are diligent in practicing each day, you should see positive changes in about three months.

Don't be disappointed or frustrated if you fall back into one of your "normal" reactions. Make note of it. This is like training for a marathon. You're not going to be perfect right away (Greenberg, https://www.psychologytoday.com/us/blog/understand

ing-narcissism/201802/7-steps-changing-your-narcissistic-responses, 2018).

Practice consideration and respect boundaries – The benefits of being aware of others' boundaries and practicing consideration is that it diminishes personal and work relationship disputes and fallouts because of boundary violations. This improves and normalizes their relationships.

Probably the most important concept for a recovering narcissist to keep in mind is to recognize where the end of their self is and where the beginning of another person begins. Practice greater consideration for the existence of other people's feelings and thoughts. Some exercises the narcissist can adopt are:

- Addressing people in both speaking and writing by name
- Listen to the same amount as you speak
- Ask appropriate questions to get to know more about other people and express sincere interest in their lives. Develop a genuine curiosity and interest of people in your life.

- Take care to not impose yourself inconsiderately into others' personal space, make use of any of their personal property, to needlessly occupying their personal time without consent.
- Ask rather than give orders when you're making a request, or assuming you know better than anyone else. Consciousness and attentiveness are necessary because narcissists are frequently good at requesting in a manipulative manner to get what they want.
- Don't ask leading questions, ask open questions. Provide space so the other person can exercise their free choice and show respect for their choice even if it's not what you want every time.

Develop substance – There is an enormous amount of benefit in developing and delivering substance. It diminishes the anxiety, stress and moral conflict that develops with pretending, lying, cheating, exaggerating, demeaning, manipulating, breaking promises, and cutting corners acknowledging deep down that you are really not the person you pretend to be.

Another benefit in developing substance is the increase in having the ability to enjoy true, genuine, durable personal and professional relationships. Build a reputation as someone who is dependable, reliable and solid. Grow trust with others from which many long-lasting personal and professional opportunities, contacts and successes can occur.

Practical pointers to achieve this are:

- Keep promises, appointments, and agreements and follow through with what you say you're going to do.
- If you can't keep any promises, don't make any.
- If you're not able to follow through, take responsibility and be accountable. Provide a solution and ascertain what you will be doing to remedy the situation going forward. This will show you are being proactive while you build trust with your integrity and honor.
- Avoid any decisions or actions that affect others to feel cheated, used, manipulated and disappointed. Focusing on making these changes

will create a measurable difference in your relationships and your work.

- Delivering what you initially promised and whether they like your substance enough to have a recurrence of the interaction again is a good way to measure whether people are happy with what you submitted. (Ni, 2014)

Increase mindfulness and use be observant – Being mindful of others diminishes conflict, friction, and misunderstandings. Social interactions increase and are more constructive.

Being observant helps increase awareness and is a useful resource to help increase awareness in many situations. Observation is the part of your awareness that uses mindfulness and aids you to make considerate and intelligent decisions.

When considering your relationships with people and you feel that your narcissistic leanings could get the better of you, ask yourself some questions:

- How will others receive what I'm about to say? How will it come off?

- How will someone feel by my behavior and communications with them? How will they feel receiving it?

- How will the other person feel slighted, feel devalued or ignored when they're on the receiving end of my behavior?

- Are my actions and words giving the impression how unique, special, superior, and great I am?

- Whenever we are observant and attentive to behaviors with others, we're taking a beneficial look in the mirror which can aid in our being seen as more human and authentic.

Seek support and help – Seeking support from a professional medical specialist who deals with mental disorders will guide you through the labyrinth of the awareness, increase belonging, diminish struggling in isolation, and begin the healing process.

It is often lonely being a pathological narcissist. They usually have a few really close relationships. Talking about the insecurities and inner struggles with the people in your life.

In order to be successful in pursuing help with this personality condition, seeking the guidance of a qualified therapist to help guide you and work with you, as well as seeking out support groups led by an experienced mental health professional is the best way to get the correct kind of aid you need.

Getting help is a brave step and these steps require resolution, will have its bumps in the road along the way but can eventually be rewarding and gratifying.

Your self-discovery is an incredible journey and you don't have to go it alone. There is a help to fulfill your needs.

Self-Forgiveness – Allows the process of healing and self-acceptance. When there can an increase in self-awareness by a narcissist, there may be a period of accompanying a sense of remorse or regret realizing the damage they've inflicted on themselves and others. You may feel that you've been a bad person and wallow in self-pity.

These moments are when you need to be kind and gentle with yourself, acknowledging that what you did was your coping mechanism to survive, that going through when your own normal growth processes were deprived in your early life.

You have an opportunity to avoid replicating your past mistakes and create a happier life with healthier relationships with yourself and others.

To further your healing and growth, speak openly with your therapist.

Getting back to humanity – Your self-help and psychological work will bring you greater truthfulness, genuine relationships, and lasting success.

The best part about all the work you put into self-discovery is that you begin seeing a sound process of getting back to humanity as an authentic person having the ability to develop healthy and genuine loving relationships. Professional and personal achievements may accomplish bigger and long lasting success.

The most important part of finding your road back to humanity is that you know that as you continue to grow and learn, you'll realize your better self and you'll be comfortable and happier with yourself (Ni, 2014).

Chapter 12: Narcissism and Therapy

Narcissistic personality disorder has been an extremely difficult pathological mental disorder to treat with therapy. Part of the reason for this is the personality traits of a narcissist.

People who are narcissists are not all the same. Treatment varies from one individual to another.

When a person with NPD enters treatment that is against their will, treatment will probably not work. However, if the therapist is adept enough to persuade the narcissist to see how their personality disorder is undermining the narcissist's relationships, quality of life, or their inability of being successful because of lost opportunities directly related to their disorder, it may be the motivation that is needed for their client to stay.

People with NPD can and do change, but only if they're willing to work through the process and put in significant effort.

Narcissism Statistics

Few people with NPD seek treatment and even when they do, they may not be willing to admit the having narcissistic personality traits or symptoms.

Currently, the rate of people with NPD in the United States is 6.2 percent and designates that narcissism is more common in men than women.

Categories of Behavior – these categories of behavior by a narcissistic person may cause them to exhibit many of the narcissism symptoms:

- Fantasies and preoccupation of power, fame, and extreme success
- Lack of Empathy
- Does not tolerate criticism
- Attention seeking for the admiration and affirmation that is needed on a constant basis
- Strong sense of entitlement
- Setting unrealistic goals
- Envy of others, especially their achievements, or their belief others should envy them
- Megalomaniacal tendencies and inflated sense of self
- The belief they are unique, special
- Difficulty in maintaining healthy relationships
- Disregard for the needs of others

Narcissism

Understanding the personality condition - In order to treat an individual who is a narcissist, they must first understand the personality disorder they have. The therapist they choose to help guide them through the therapy process must be a specialist on what is means to be in a narcissistic relationship with narcissistic traits.

Unfortunately, although there are therapists who are good in guiding a normal person through the therapy process, there are those therapists who do not have an inkling how exciting, stimulating yet destructive life is with a narcissistic person.

Remember that a *sense of entitlement, lack of insight and lack of empathy* are the three major trains of narcissism.

Building a therapeutic alliance – A therapist develops a therapeutic relationship which is a consistent and close association that exists to help the person in therapy change their life for the better.

The therapist must require two things from a person who has narcissistic tendencies and forming a therapeutic relationship with this person—collaboration and respect.

People with narcissism present a challenge for a therapist to develop a close association in therapy. Respect for and collaboration with others is a tremendous challenge for a narcissist. Some might say this would be virtually impossible in some severe cases.

The relationship between the therapist and the narcissist will be in a learning mode. The narcissist will be developing their relationship in real time and the narcissist will be practicing interpersonal abilities with their therapist.

Identifying the defenses – The therapist must try to help the narcissist identify some of the personality modes that they've used as protective shields throughout their life.

Some common examples of these personality modes or personas are:

- Critic
- Abuser
- Manipulator

- Superior one
- Judge
- Addict
- Womanizer
- Detached persona
- Entitled
- Victim
- Bored one
- Rager

Therapists will work with each person individually to identify which of these and many other personas they have used and are their unique defenses.

The personas listed above that people with narcissism adopt as their emotional protection. Two of the feelings narcissists seem to avoid and are missing from the psychological makeup are *vulnerability* and *neediness*.

Underlying triggers – In the last chapter, a narcissist's triggers were touched upon and identified as what sets narcissists bad behavior patterns off. They are what cause the need for a narcissist to have protective personas. The reasons that the triggers are activated are called schemas and can be thought to be like a trigger that is activated when pushed like buttons and causes a "narcissistic wound."

Some triggers that are experienced by narcissists and their feelings:

- Inner defectiveness
- Emotional abandonment
- Emotional deprivation
- Lack of security or control
- Afraid of shame or ridicule

Identifying the underlying triggers are difficult to identify because you are working with a client who may be emotionally blocked or split off from feeling these devastating emotions and vulnerability. They also may have low insight.

Before you will give an identity to the underlying root of the problem, you will more likely be greeted by a protective mode.

Realize that the main emotional experience that a narcissist is trying to avoid is a sense of shame. The person flips into their protective mode rather than have an experience where they feel a sense of shame.

In order for the narcissist to manage these underlying feelings of shame, teaching self-compassion, and providing self-soothing strategies that are healthy will help them through this process.

Most narcissists has an inner hurt child. The inner child is reacting and responding to the early trauma as a child.

The narcissist was not emotionally regulated properly in the inter-relationship with their parent(s). This lack of emotional regulation may have caused the child to split off and to protect their inner sense of shame developed protective personas for their self-defense.

Interest in Narcissistic Personality Disorder

Today there is an abundance of interest in NPD and the easy accessibility of information about it on the Internet.

More people today recognize that they are narcissists and are seeking help from qualified therapists who can help them be diagnosed. These are self-aware narcissists who are likely candidates to receive psychotherapy (Greenberg P. E., 2019).

Self-Aware Narcissists and their characteristics are:

Motivated – this person wants to change what's going on in their life that they don't like. It could be they're not doing as well in their career as they would like, or their marriage is failing. If there was nothing wrong of note the would not be seeking therapy

Psychologically minded – People who do well in psychotherapy have an interest in people and wonder how people behave and think. They have the capacity to be truly interested in why people are the way they are.

Narcissists who are psychologically minded will most likely follow through with their therapy longer than others because they like the self-discovery process.

Have the capacity for self-reflection – Most narcissists are too busy to persuade themselves and everybody else how they are perfect to ever seek therapy and look within themselves for the source and/or resolution. Instead, they use their energy in finding clever ways to place blame on other people and tell them they need to change.

The capacity for self-reflection is the ability to look at one's own motives and behaviors objectively and have a willingness to do so. There are only a handful of narcissists from thousands willing to self-reflect voluntarily and anxious enough to do so.

High intelligence – People who are highly intelligent are more than likely to view the "big picture" and have the ability to understand the difference between their perceptions of who they are and the reality of who they are.

High functioning – People who are able to direct their everyday life without major difficulty. The have the ability to initiate projects and complete them. They have a job, graduated school, and have a stable living environment. They have the ability to make friends.

People who are too low functioning will exert all their energy on just surviving. They are more concerned about how and where they'll get their next meal and what they'll do about their latest eviction notice than they will much think to their diagnosis (Greenberg P. E., 2019).

Ego strength – Having ego strength is thought to have the capability to maintain one's emotional stability and be in touch with reality while you're under external or internal stress.

Being in therapy is a little like having your house remodeled. You'll have mess, chaos, and uncertainty while the remodeling is being done. While the remodeling is happening, a person needs strong internal support to get through the process. So too when a narcissist is i therapy. While they are going through the process, they need to have an abundance of internal support that is strong so when their therapist challenges one of their narcissistic defenses, the entire edifice doesn't collapse.

Many narcissists have trouble sustaining their functioning when they have their narcissistic tendencies and masks removed and they connect with their underlying shame.

Dismantling a narcissist's view needs to be done very carefully and slowly.
The psychotherapy of narcissistic disorders takes a long time because of how slowly the therapist and their client have to dismantle their psyche to bring them to their true reality. The slowness of the process is why many narcissists quit therapy before they can achieve significant goals.

The therapist has to make sure that their client is learning and beginning to use new coping mechanisms that are healthy and beneficial for their client before the therapist asks the client to discard all the narcissistic ones.

Considering the narcissist's coping mechanisms have been ingrained since childhood, the ability to give them up for the healthier ones can possibly be more difficult than the client and the therapist imagined. For the narcissist, they have become almost like a security blanket.

If the therapist sees the possibility to switch to new coping tools are not yet possible, the number of therapy sessions per week will need to be increased. *This will allow the therapist to loan the client their ego strength* that the client can draw from while they go through the delicate and difficult transitional process (Greenberg P. E., 2019).

The desire for self-improvement – Within the many people who are afflicted with a narcissistic personality disorder, there is a subset of those people who want to evolve, and are willing to do the work in order to accomplish their goal of a healthy mental life.

These people are frequently the same type of people who sign up to learn a new language or investigate how to sign up for classes on topics they had wanted to study in college and didn't.

These are clients who believe that change is possible. They have the ability to envision themselves growing and changing.

Narcissism Treatment – Therapy is considered the most effective treatment for narcissism. Therapy focuses on two components of NPD—the patient's emotions and beliefs, such as superiority or entitlement and the behaviors that are associated with narcissism.

A person with NPD is aided in understanding how their emotions affect their behavior. Once the behaviors and identified, a therapist can work set goals for behavior changes with a client.

Helping a person with a narcissistic personality disorder to heal is one that can be challenging for both the client and the therapist.

There are some people with narcissistic tendencies who make better candidates to receive psychotherapy than others. Generally, people with NPD who show motivation, intelligent psychologically minded and are high functioning have the capacity for good ego strength, self-reflections, and an interest in working towards self-improvement. They are more than likely to garner enjoyment from their therapy and stay with it to achieve significant improvements (Greenberg P. E., 2019).

Conclusion

Thank for reading Narcissistic Personality Disorder: A Self Help Recovery Emotional Guide to Understand the Causes of Narcissism and How to Survive Narcissistic Abuse in Any Kind of Relationship to the end.

Many people don't read through an entire book. They are initially intrigued by the title and the description of its content and begin to read it. Then some distraction has them put it down and move on to other activities.

It seems you are serious about learning about narcissistic personality disorder and its effects on the people who suffer from it as well as the people who suffer from being in abusive relationships with a person with this type of disorder.

The book effectively teaches those who have never been aware of this personality disorder. It also outlines the signs and symptoms of the disorder and how it affects people they come in contact on a daily basis.

Before you read this book, you may have thought that NPD was not a very serious disorder and the most a narcissist have been self-centered and talk about themselves constantly. What was not known is how this personality can be destructive to people who have to deal with them. Now you have learned more about this personality disorder and understand its effects on others, as well as how a person can become involved with them.

Hopefully, this book is informative as well as a guide and will send me an email to let me know how you've benefited from this book.

Printed in Great Britain
by Amazon